Hungary

Hungary

BY RUTH BJORKLUND

Enchantment of the World™
Second Series

CHILDREN'S PRESS®

An Imprint of Scholastic Inc.

Frontispiece: **Matthias Church, Budapest**

Consultant: Lynn Hooker, Associate Professor, Central Eurasian Studies, Indiana University–Bloomington

Please note: All statistics are as up-to-date as possible at the time of publication.

Book production by The Design Lab

Library of Congress Cataloging-in-Publication Data
Bjorklund, Ruth.
 Hungary / by Ruth Bjorklund.
  pages cm — (Enchantment of the world)
 Includes bibliographic references and index.
 ISBN 978-0-531-23295-8 (library binding)
 1. Hungary—Juvenile literature. I. Title.
 DB906.B54 2016
 943.9—dc23   2015021148

1 2 3 4 5 6 7 8 9 10 R 25 24 23 22 21 20 19 18 17 16

Budapest

Contents

Left to right: **Budapest, Veszprém, fallow deer, friends, traditional dancing**

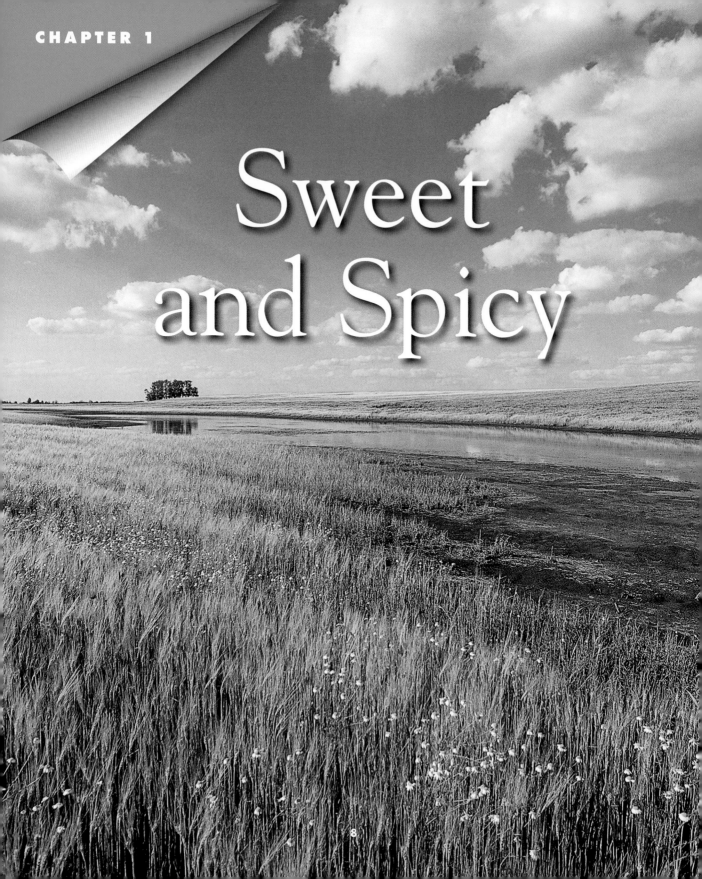

CHAPTER 1

Sweet and Spicy

JÁNOS LIVES IN A REGION CALLED THE GREAT Hungarian Plain. It covers nearly one-half of the central European nation of Hungary. In particular, János lives in the southeastern part of the Great Hungarian Plain, where there are vast grasslands and marshes that people call the *puszta*, meaning "wasteland." The Tisza River flows through the puszta and often floods the grasslands, making the soil fertile. More than a thousand years ago, some of the earliest people to settle in what is now Hungary began farming on the puszta. Like his family's ancestors, János's family grows paprika, a sweet red pepper that is uniquely Hungarian. It is a spice prized by chefs around the world.

In the middle of the twentieth century, the Soviet Union, a large communist nation to the east, began to dominate Hungary. Under communism, the government owns the businesses and controls the economy. A communist government was established in Hungary. The new rulers quickly turned much of the puszta farmland into large farmers' collectives

Opposite: **The Great Hungarian Plain stretches across more than half the land in Hungary.**

HUNGARY

- ● Cities of over 120,000 people
- ○ Other cities
- ✪ National capital

0   60 miles

0   60 kilometers

SLOVAKIA

UKRAINE

AUSTRIA

SLOVENIA

CROATIA

SERBIA

ROMANIA

Aggtelek National Park

Sárospatak
Kazincbarcika
Szerencs
Kisvárda
Balassagyarmat
Ózd
Miskolc
Nyíregyháza
Mátészalka
Hollókő
Salgótarján
Mosonmagyaróvár
Eger
Tiszavasvári
Esztergom
Visegrád
Gyöngyös
Mezőkövesd
Hajdúnánás
Nyírbátor
Sopron
Vác
Hatvan
Heves
Tiszafüred
Balmazújváros
Kapuvár
Csorna
Győr
Komárom
Gödöllő
Hortobágy National Park
Debrecen
Tatabánya
Budapest
Jászberény
Hajdúszoboszló
Kőszeg
Pápa
Mór
Érd
Monor
Karcag
Püspökladány
Zirc
Szombathely
Sárvár
Székesfehérvár
Dabas
Cegléd
Szolnok
Törökszentmiklós
Berettyóújfalu
Ajka
Veszprém
Mezőtúr
Szeghalom
Körmend
Balatonfüred
Dunaújváros
Tiszakécske
Gyomaendrőd
Zalaegerszeg
Tapolca
Siófok
Kecskemét
Kunszentmárton
Szarvas
Sarkad
Keszthely
Tab
Sárbogárd
Békéscsaba
Lake Balaton
Paks
Kiskőrös
Szentes
Marcali
Kalocsa
Oroszháza
Nagykanizsa
Kaposvár
Dombóvár
Kiskunhalas
Hódmezővásárhely
Nagyatád
Szekszárd
Szeged
Makó
Szigetvár
Barcs
Pécs
Baja
Mohács
Siklós

Danube R.

Tisza R.

N   E   S   W

Hungary

owned by the government. Farmworkers had to sell their crops to the government at low prices. People who opposed the communist government were sent to the farmers' collectives and forced to work in the fields.

In 1990, the communist rule ended and the giant collective farms were divided up. If they could afford it, farmers bought small pieces of land. But times were difficult and many people did not have enough money to buy even basic things, so they left the farms and moved to the nearby cities of Kalocsa or Debrecen to work.

János's grandfather bought 5 acres (2 hectares) of land. Today the farm is owned by János's parents and aunt and uncle. His father grew up working on the farm, and János and his cousins are expected to help when they are not in school. Growing perfect Hungarian paprika is a demanding task. Paprika needs long, hot summers and just a small amount of rain to grow well. On small paprika farms like the one that belongs to János's family, almost everything is done by hand. János and his cousins must help during planting season. Winters are cold, and in years when there is a lot of snow they plant the seeds under glass

Paprika peppers dry outside a house in Hungary. Once the peppers are dry, they can be ground into paprika.

frames near the house. This helps protect the seeds from the weather but lets the sunlight reach them. The paprika peppers sprout there and grow into little plants that are transferred into the fields in May. Other years, they plant the seeds directly into the ground in March. Traditionally, farmers plant the peppers on March 12—Saint Gergely's (Gregory's) name day. There is a saint for every day of the year. János's uncle, whose name is Gergely, complains that he always has to work on his name day, instead of having a party like everyone else.

The paprika peppers need to ripen on the vine and be picked at just the right time. Picking the peppers is done by hand. It is grueling work, bending over all day. János's parents and aunt and uncle appreciate when he and his cousins help after school. After the peppers are picked, they are dried for a few weeks to get the best flavor and color in order to command the best price. János's grandmother wins the top prize every year for her goulash stew in the goulash competition held during the Kalocsa Paprika Festival. She boasts that her goulash is always the sweetest and the reddest. Hungarian paprika is so sweet that it is an ingredient in many Hungarian desserts.

Summer Break

Every summer, János and his family visit with friends and relatives. This June, his cousins are visiting his village in time to go to the Equestrian Days fair at the nearby Hortobágy National Park. The park covers vast grasslands and wetlands. János's cousin competes in horse shows, and this festival has one of the biggest horse shows of the year. János's favorite events feature the *csikóses*—the

cowboys of the puszta. For hundreds of years, the csikóses herded cattle across the plains. The cowboys were frequently attacked by raiding armies as they herded, so they learned many daring skills to protect their animals. During the festival, the csikóses show off their legendary stunts, such as doing handstands in the saddle or standing and riding on two horses at once.

This year, before the autumn paprika harvest, János and his parents are going to drive to the other end of the country to spend a week with friends in a cottage near Lake Balaton. At nearly 60 miles (97 kilometers) long, it is the largest lake in central Europe and has long been a popular resort area. At home, János likes to swim in pools and fish in the Tisza River, but he has never been in a sailboat or paddled a canoe, which he will finally get to do at the lake. His parents are looking forward to seeing their friends and going out to restaurants

Paprika is an important ingredient in goulash, the Hungarian national dish. Hungarian paprika is highly valued because it is often stronger and sweeter than paprika from other countries, without having too much hot spice.

People enjoy a night out in Budapest.

and clubs to hear music and dance. Their village at home is small and does not have much entertainment.

While János likes his village and has many close friends, he really likes visiting Budapest. He plans to go to college there in a few years. Millions of people live in and around Budapest, making it an exciting city. János's cousins laugh at him for wanting to come to the city for vacations. Most people in Budapest prefer to leave and go to the country to go cycling, swimming, and horseback riding. But János has his favorite Budapest destinations, such as Buda Castle and the Hungarian Natural History Museum. Buda Castle is an ancient historic castle on a hill overlooking Budapest and the Danube River. The natural history museum displays fossils of ancient humans who once roamed across Hungary. It also has an amazing dinosaur garden. Budapest has many historic buildings and great restaurants. It also has more than a hundred thermal (warm-water) pools. Some are ancient pools surrounded by marble columns and statues that were built by the early Romans and Ottoman Turks. János likes the park at Palatinus Strand because there are so many pools there and two of them have water slides and a wave machine. His cousin's favorite is the Széchenyi Baths, which has eighteen pools. Some of them are steam baths or mineral baths for healing, and some are big lap-swimming pools. János's cousin's favorite is the large warm-water pool with floating chessboards. Many people in Budapest are avid chess players, and the world's top woman chess player, Judit Polgár, is from Budapest. János and his cousins differ about what makes for a more exciting vacation or more interesting place to live, but they all agree that their country is a special place to explore.

Men play chess while soaking in a thermal pool on a chilly night in Budapest.

CHAPTER 2

In the Heart of a Continent

HUNGARY LIES NEAR THE CENTER OF THE EUROPEAN continent. Mountains and hills ring the country while rivers, lakes, and plains extend across its interior. Hungary boasts fertile soils, leafy forests, and a magnificent array of interesting landforms, many of which lie underground.

Opposite: **Much of western Hungary consists of rolling hills.**

New Borders

For the last two thousand years, Hungary has been a battleground. Because of conquest and war, the nation's borders changed many times. Today, Hungary borders seven countries. Slovakia lies to the north and Ukraine to the northeast. To the east is a long border with Romania. Serbia and Croatia are to the south, and Slovenia and Austria are to the west. Hungary, which has no coastline, has a land area of 35,919 square miles (93,030 square kilometers), making it about the size of the U.S. state of Indiana.

The Bakony Mountains are flat-topped. Much of the forest that once covered the mountains has been cleared to make way for agriculture.

Plains, Hills, and Valleys

Nearly two-thirds of Hungary is made up of gently rolling plains and river basins. The two main basins are the Great Hungarian Plain, in the east, and the Little Hungarian Plain, in the northwest.

The Great Hungarian Plain covers much of the country. It is largely treeless, but it has rich and fertile soil. The Little Hungarian Plain lies just north of Lake Balaton, the largest lake in Hungary and in all of central Europe. Its terrain is similar to that of the Great Hungarian Plain, but it receives slightly more rainfall.

Along part of Hungary's western border with Austria, the foothills of the Alps Mountains cast shadows over the valleys and plains. In the west is a region of plains and rolling hills called Transdanubia (meaning "past the Danube," the region's major river). In the south, the Transdanubian Hills rise to form a low forest-covered range called the Mecsek Hills. This area is a karst landscape, rugged land made of limestone rock carved by rain and water to form deep ridges, caves, and sinkholes. The area features beautiful forests and streams. Northern Transdanubia was once covered by a sea called the Pannonian Sea. Jutting out of what was once the sea are volcanic mountains, called the Bakony Mountains, which also feature karst formations. The Bakony Mountains eroded over time and are now rounded. They rise to about 1,950 to 2,300 feet (600 to 700 meters) above sea level. Several streams run underground, and in some areas the earth opens up, giving a glimpse of the partially hidden streams. The openings are called karstic windows.

The Mátra and Bükk mountain ranges run across most of northeastern Hungary. They are part of the foothills of the Carpathian Mountains, Europe's second-longest mountain chain. The country's highest peak, Mount Kékes, rises 3,330 feet (1,015 m) in the Mátra Mountains. The Bükk Mountains are noted for their steep cliffs, caves, rugged karst, and lush beech forests.

The River Is Wide

Two major rivers, the Tisza and the Danube, nourish Hungary. The headwaters of the Tisza River are in the Carpathian Mountains in Ukraine. Once the river reaches the Hungarian border, it flows for nearly 600 miles (950 km) in a large sweeping loop, first northward and then southwest across the Great Hungarian Plain. The Tisza eventually joins the Danube River, Europe's second-longest river.

A Look at Hungary's Cities

Budapest, Hungary's capital, is also the nation's largest city, with an estimated population of 1,744,665 in 2014. The eastern city of Debrecen (below) is the second-largest city in the country, home to 203,914 people. The city is a commercial and cultural center in the Great Hungarian Plain. Centuries ago, Debrecen prospered from salt mining, farming, and cattle ranching. In the 1500s, it became the center of the Calvinist Protestant religion in Hungary. The Protestants established a college in 1538, which eventually turned into the University of Debrecen, now the oldest continuously operating college in Hungary. Debrecen's towering Great Reformed Church is the largest Protestant church in Hungary. During the Hungarian Revolution of 1848, the country's lawmakers fled Budapest and quietly met in the church.

Szeged, which had a population of 161,921 in 2014, is the third-largest city in the country and the largest city in the south. It is a center for higher education. Many of

its residents are students or teachers at the University of Szeged, which serves thirty thousand students. Szeged has a reputation as a pleasant city, where visitors and residents alike enjoy tree-lined streets, thermal pools, concerts, operas, folk festivals, and sports events.

Hungary's fourth-largest city, Miskolc, is home to 161,265 people. It is an industrial city in the northeastern part of the country. Major industries today include the manufacture of cement and glass, as well as food processing. The city has several well-preserved buildings, such as Castle Diósgyőr and the Old Wooden Church.

Pécs (above), Hungary's fifth-largest city with a population of 146,581, is located in the Transdanubia region. The city has a diverse history, which is evident in its architecture. There are Roman ruins, Catholic cathedrals, and Turkish baths and mosques. Located at the base of the Mecsek Hills, Pécs was long an industrial mining town. Today, it is known for its many festivals, museums, art galleries, shops, restaurants, and historical sites. The city is near enough to the Mediterranean Sea to have a warm, moist climate that helps nut and fruit trees to thrive. The city is a center for growing almonds and wine grapes.

The Danube begins its course in the Black Forest Mountains of western Germany and collects water from nearly three hundred tributaries before emptying into the Black Sea. The Danube enters Hungary through the Hungarian Gates Gorge, on the border with Slovakia. After passing swiftly through this canyon, the river slows down and widens. Over time, the Danube has deposited rocks and silt, forming two large islands, one in Slovakia and one in Hungary. Combined, these large islands are home to nearly two hundred thousand people. Farther downstream, the Danube crosses the Little Hungarian Plain and flows toward

Hills rise from the banks of the Danube in northern Hungary.

Going Underground

Hungary has one of the largest cave systems in Europe, much to the delight of spelunkers—people who explore caves. Both the Mecsek and Bakony Mountains have deep karst formations, where many caves are found. The Mecsek range has numerous stream-filled caves and the Bakony Mountains have many deep, vertical caves. Near Lake Balaton is Tapolca Lake Cave, a cave with a large underground lake that can be toured by boat.

The Aggtelek National Park, on the border with Slovakia, features extremely rugged karst lands and caves. The most important is Baradla Cave (right), where streams, stalactites, and stalagmites are found throughout its 15 miles (25 km) of passageways. One section is so large that it serves as a concert hall.

Many of the largest and most impressive caves in Hungary are found in the Bükk Mountains. There, one of the deepest caves in all of Hungary, István-lápa Cave, drops 820 feet (250 m).

the capital city of Budapest. After passing Budapest, the Danube flows across the Great Hungarian Plain where it again slows, widens, and holds many small islands. Beyond the islands, other rivers join the Danube. The enlarged Danube then races through another gorge, called the Iron Gate, with a tremendous torrent.

Warm Water

Thanks to volcanic action long ago and mountains of limestone rock, Hungary has more than 1,000 hot springs, also known as thermal springs. Thermal springs occur when rainwater falls on soft limestone rock and burrows to greater depths, where the temperature is warmer. The recent fallen water pushes the older, warmed water up through channels in the limestone. Many of Hungary's thermal springs occur in caves. The springs can be as warm as 90 degrees Fahrenheit (32 degrees Celsius).

Some of the springs feed lakes, where the water temperature stays warm enough to allow swimming throughout the year. Lake Hévíz, the largest thermal lake in Europe, is near Lake Balaton and covers 13 acres (5 ha), which is the size of about ten football fields. The springs feeding it are so active that the entire lake refills with warm, fresh water every three days.

Climate

Hungary has what is known as a continental climate, meaning that the country does not suffer from extreme weather conditions caused by oceans. The weather is somewhat predictable as a result. Each season has a distinct feature—snow in winter, flowers in spring, heat in summer, and color in autumn. The

Healing Waters

The capital city of Budapest is known as the City of Healing Waters. Beneath the city lie more than one hundred caves and thermal lakes and springs. The caves extend in long, winding passages lined with striking formations, where rock seems to be oozing down from the ceiling. Budapest's longest cave, the Pálvölgyi Cave, extends for 11 miles (18 km).

A biker crosses a bridge on a snowy day in Budapest. Snowfall is common in the winter in Budapest, but it is usually light.

coldest month is January, where days of 0°F (–18°C) are common. At night, the temperatures fall even lower. Mountain areas can be extremely cold. The nation's record low temperature is –31°F (–35°C) in the Mátra Mountains. The warmest summer month is July, when the temperature often tops 80°F (27°C). The highest temperature ever recorded in Hungary was 107°F (42°C) on July 20, 2007, in Kiskunhalas, a city in the south. Spring and autumn are the rainiest times in Hungary, although sudden thunderstorms sometimes occur in summer, and precipitation in the form of snow falls in winter.

Hungary's Geographic Features

Area: 35,919 square miles (93,030 sq km)

Highest Elevation: Mount Kékes, 3,330 feet (1,015 m) above sea level

Lowest Elevation: Near Szeged, 259 feet (79 m) above sea level

Greatest Distance East–West: 312 miles (502 km)

Greatest Distance North–South: 193 miles (311 km)

Longest River: Tisza River, 360 miles (579 km) long

Largest Lake: Lake Balaton, 232 square miles (601 sq km)

Average Low Temperature: In Budapest, 25°F (−4°C) in January, 69°F (20°C) in July

Average High Temperature: In Budapest, 34°F (1°C) in January, 80°F (27°C) in July

Average Annual Precipitation: In Budapest, 23 inches (59 cm)

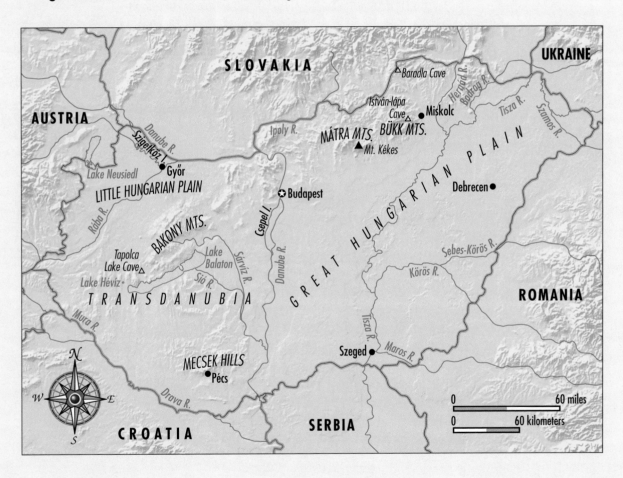

CHAPTER 3

Wild World

ALTHOUGH HUNGARY IS A SMALL COUNTRY, IT IS home to a large number of plant and animal species. A temperate climate and a variety of landscapes have created many habitats where plants and animals thrive. The natural features of the country—mountains, plains, forests, marshlands, lakes, and rivers—are a haven for many birds, wildlife, fish, flowers, trees, and grasses.

Opposite: **Fallow deer race across a field in southeastern Hungary. These deer are quick, sometimes running about 30 miles (50 km) per hour.**

Habitats

Hungary can be divided into three habitat regions. The first is the plains, which support some trees but are mostly covered with grasses, meadow flowers, and brush. These plains are home to many species of birds, insects, butterflies, and small mammals. The second large habitat region is the mountains, which feature many caves, karst landscapes, and forests, and have wildlife in abundance. Lastly, the Tisza and Danube Rivers and numerous streams and lakes provide many aquatic environments that attract birds, amphibians, and fish.

The Eurasian eagle-owl is considered the most powerful species of owl. Its common prey includes rabbits, hedgehogs, and rats.

In Flight

About four hundred species of birds either are native to Hungary or nest there while on their migrations. The Hortobágy National Park was created to protect 343 species of birds on the Great Hungarian Plain. From the large Eurasian eagle-owl to the tiniest of hummingbirds, the variety is stunning.

In Hungary's forests are many species of owls that hunt at night for insects, moles, voles, shrews, snakes, and frogs. The Eurasian eagle-owl, one of the world's largest owl species, sometimes catches and feasts on squirrels, hares, geese, and foxes. Other forest-dwelling raptors, or birds of prey, include the eastern imperial eagle and the rough-legged hawk. Smaller birds also share Hungary's forested mountain lands, including waxwings, thrushes, nuthatches, chickadees, shrikes, and nine species of woodpeckers.

The vast meadows and fields on the plains invite birds of all types. Many kinds of raptors hunt in the lowlands, including buzzards, vultures, barn owls, eagles, falcons, peregrines, and harriers. Nesting in grasses and flitting over fields are jays, crows, flycatchers, and many songbirds, such as warblers, sparrows, and larks.

Hungary's lakes and rivers are teeming with birds and waterfowl. Ducks, geese, and swans swim on the surface, while chattering kingfishers hunt along the shore. Marshes are a perfect feeding ground for graceful herons and cranes. Each year, nearly one hundred thousand cranes migrate on their long journey from Africa into Hungary, where they stop to rest and feed in shallow lakes. Another summer visitor is the stately black stork, a wading bird that stands more than 3 feet tall (1 m).

Big Bird

The national bird of Hungary is the great bustard, the largest land bird in Europe. The male weighs up to 30 pounds (14 kilograms) and has a wingspan of 8 feet (2.5 m). The great bustard is found throughout Hungary, mainly along the Tisza and sometimes along the Danube River. The great bustard is a shy bird except during the mating season, when it turns into a big show-off. Then, the male dances and struts, flaunting its feathers. The highlight of his display is when he tips himself upside down to expose his white tail feathers to the sun. The white feathers sparkle in the light, attracting female great bustards.

Hungary is home to 150 species of butterflies—many more than are in neighboring countries. Flower-filled meadows near the forest edge are the perfect spot for butterflies to gather. Butterflies such as the large purple emperor and the duke of Burgundy are rarely seen in other parts of Europe but are common in Hungary. In addition, several species of butterflies that are threatened or endangered around the world can be found in healthy populations in Hungary, including the dusky large blue butterfly, the woodland brown, and the clouded Apollo.

Fish

Warm lake waters and shallow rivers yield a bounty of aquatic plants and algae, providing plenty of food for big, plant-eating carps that abound in Hungary. The largest native Hungarian carp weighs between 65 and 100 pounds (30 and 50 kg). Another species, the grass carp, can eat 100 to 120 percent of its body weight daily. Most carnivorous (meat-eating) fish live in the swift-moving, oxygen-rich rivers and large lakes. These include fish such as the northern pike, which has two rows of teeth. The largest Hungarian fish is the wels catfish, which can grow to 6.5 feet (2 m) long. Other varieties of fish found in Hungary include trout, perch, and the highly prized food fish called the zander (also known as the pike perch).

Reptiles and Amphibians

Hungary has an abundance of wetlands, which provide the perfect habitat for amphibians. There are so many frogs there, that the sound of their croaking can be deafening during mat-

ing season. Among the amphibians making their home in the wetlands are European tree frogs, Moor frogs, Danube crested newts, and fire-bellied toads. To scare away predators, the small fire-bellied toad exposes its red belly to indicate that it is poisonous, like many brightly colored frogs are. The fire salamander, which hunts at night and hides under leaves during the day, also uses its bright color to ward off predators.

Many reptiles are also found in Hungary. Lizards, such as the large green lizard, which feasts on wild berries, worms, caterpillars, and snails, are common. The European pond turtle is the only native turtle in Hungary. It is found in many wetland areas, although its numbers are decreasing. Humans and predators devour turtle eggs and many of the shallow, stagnant ponds where turtles live are polluted. Hungary has a variety of snake species. These include some venomous snakes, such as the long-nosed viper and the meadow viper. But the country is also

The long-nosed viper is the most dangerous snake in Europe. Its bite can be fatal to humans.

home to many more grass snakes, such as the dice snake, that are harmless to humans. They eat frogs, tadpoles, and small fish.

Mammals

Small mammals live in all regions of Hungary. These animals include hares, dormice, rats, moles, pikas, squirrels, and hamsters. With so many caves, Hungary supports many bat species, including the pond bat, the bent-wing bat, and the greater noctule, Europe's largest bat and one of the rarest. Red foxes hunt in both lowlands and highlands. Other lowland predators in Hungary include the ermine, polecat, beaver, badger, weasel, otter, wolverine, and European mink.

Loved to Death

The European mink is a long, sausage-shaped animal in the weasel family that lives near streams and ponds. It has short legs, a pointed snout, a short bushy tail, webbed feet, and a very thick, soft, and shiny coat of blackish-brown fur. The mink hunts at night both on land and in water, feeding on birds, voles, frogs, fish, small ducks, and insects. Male minks are much larger than females and are usually able to fend off any predators that mink families might encounter. However, the European mink has not been successful in fending off one major predator—humans. In the eleventh century, royalty began wearing furs such as mink, and in the centuries after, mink fur became a status symbol. Trappers hunted the animals nearly to extinction. The European mink is now listed as critically endangered. The few European mink that are still found in the wild live mostly along the shores of the Danube in Hungary.

Hortobágy National Park is located in the grasslands, called puszta, of the Large Hungarian Plain. The park is devoted to protecting the descendants of ancient animals that once roamed Hungary. Although some of these ancient species have been domesticated, the park's protected animals have kept their ancient genetic makeup. Wild horses, called Przewalski's horses (left), run free, as do wolves and jackals. Other animals that live in the park include Hungarian gray cattle, which have long, curving horns, Mangalica pigs, which have red curly coats, and Racka sheep, which have spiraling horns and long, tangled fur. Hungarian herders manage the livestock and protect them from predators.

Most of Hungary's large mammals live in the colder forests and the karst regions of the highlands. The creatures include wolves, brown bears, deer, wild boars, jackals, and lynx. Historically, Hungarians were highly skilled hunters, and over time, they overhunted these animals. In the last six decades, pollution and habitat destruction have also decreased the number of mammals. But today, Hungarians are working to protect their wildlife, and the population of large mammals is now on the rise.

Trees, Plants, and Flowers

Much of Hungary was once covered with forest, but trees were cut to clear land for farming and to be used as construction materials and as fuel. Today, only 20 percent of Hungary is forested. Only 10 percent of the land supports native forest; the

Peonies come in many colors, including pink, red, white, and yellow.

rest of the forests were planted. Most of the trees in Hungary's forests are deciduous, meaning they lose their leaves when the weather turns cold. Broad-leafed trees such as beech, oak, locust, poplar, and willow are common.

Most of Hungary is flat or has gently rolling plains, crossed by rivers and streams. The plains have been taken over to a great extent for agricultural use, but there remains an abundance of colorful wildflowers. Nearly two thousand species of wildflowers are native to Hungary, including the Hungarian daisy, the blue poppy, the lilac, and the early blooming Hungarian crocus. Hungary is noted for its beautiful peonies, which have lush leaves and big, showy blooms. Although peonies are grown in gardens everywhere, 90 percent of all the world's wild peonies grow in Hungary.

National Flower

The national flower of Hungary is the red tulip. The color red has long been a symbol of love and good fortune. Many Hungarian folktales feature red tulips, and Hungarian folk art pieces such as painted furniture, pottery, and embroidered fabrics are frequently decorated with red tulips.

The Environment

People in the region of Hungary have been enjoying its wealth of natural resources for two thousand years, and the environment is now suffering. The problems come from many sources—population growth, increased agricultural needs, and industry. All of these have led to the loss of forests, decreased wildlife, and air and water pollution.

Clear-cut logging has damaged the land in Hungary and destroyed the habitat of many animals.

Forests are logged for their valuable timber to supply building materials. The forests are also cleared to make room for more agriculture. When forests are cut, wild animals lose their source of food and shelter, and many cannot survive.

Air and water pollution are complex problems that are difficult to solve. Factories, coal-burning power plants, and cars and trucks all contribute to air pollution. Waterways are also polluted. Wastewater from factories and chemical fertilizers from farms get into rivers and lakes. Additionally, rains cause flooding in mountain regions where many mines are located. The floodwaters carry toxic waste such as cyanide downstream from

Lake Balaton has been a resort area since the early 1800s.

the mines. Besides these problems, Hungary must contend with polluted water that flows in from other countries. More than 90 percent of Hungary's water originates in a foreign country, where the Hungarian government has little control.

But Hungarians are proud of their natural beauty and are working to clean up the environment and protect wildlife. In recent years, many new environmental laws have been enacted. Both international and community groups are active in educating people about pollution prevention and natural resource conservation.

Approximately 10 percent of the land in Hungary is protected by the government. Many projects are in place to plant more forests and clean the air and water. Farmers are using new and healthier methods to produce their crops. Cities have new recycling stations to reduce waste in landfills.

Air is getting cleaner. With advancements in technology, cars pollute less and factories and electric power plants are reducing emissions. Budapest, the Hungarian city with the most traffic congestion, now has an efficient public transportation system, meaning fewer cars are on the road. Additionally, more people are using bicycles to get to work or school.

Hungary also takes part in many international programs dedicated to cleaning up the waterways. Norway, for example, helped Hungary clean Lake Balaton. On June 29, 1994, Hungary and other countries signed an agreement to clean up and preserve the Danube River. Much progress has been made, and the Danube is now cleaner and healthier, and every year these fourteen countries celebrate Danube Day.

CHAPTER 4

A Turbulent History

S KULLS, BONES, AND OTHER ARTIFACTS THAT BELONGED
to early humans called Neanderthals have been discovered in
caves in Hungary. The fossils found in Hungary date back one
hundred thousand years. Neanderthals were fire builders and
big-game hunters of woolly mammoths and other large mammals. Modern humans later migrated into what is now Hungary.
Experts say that these modern humans were nomads who began
to settle in 6000 BCE in what is now the Transdanubian region.
Archaeologists have also found remnants of swords, spears,
hammers, and farm tools in the area, dating to the Bronze Age,
which lasted from about 2700 to 800 BCE in Hungary.

Opposite: **People of the
Tisza culture lived on the
Great Hungarian Plain
about 2,500 years ago.
They farmed, hunted, and
made pottery and human
figurines.**

Many Migrations

During Hungary's Bronze Age, many peaceful groups migrated
into the region. Around 800 BCE, at the end of the Bronze
Age, Persian horsemen from western Asia thundered across
the eastern plains. They were followed by a number of Celtic
groups that were in the Transdanubian region.

Beginning in the first century BCE, the powerful Roman Empire expanded into what is now Hungary from its base in southern Europe. The Romans built forts and watchtowers and established cities, some of which are Hungary's major cities today. The Romans also built roads, houses, stadiums, steam baths, and aqueducts (channels for transporting water to farms and towns). The Romans divided the region that is now Hungary into two areas: Pannonia in the west and Dacia in the east. In 271 CE, the Roman rulers abandoned Dacia.

Later, the region was overrun by Goth, Hun, and Slavic peoples. Beginning around 430 CE, Attila, the king of the Huns (a group related to Mongolian and Turkish people), set out to conquer Europe. On his military campaign to conquer the Roman Empire and other kingdoms, Attila and his armies crossed Hungary, raiding everything in their path and enslaving many survivors. For a time, Attila ruled his empire from Buda, Hungary. After his death in 453 CE, no one was fierce enough to control his empire and the conquered societies slowly broke away and began to rebuild.

Migrations and Invasions

Persians, 6th century BCE	←	Goths, 4th century CE
Celts, 4th century BCE	←	Huns, 5th century CE
Roman province, 120 CE	←	Slavs, 6th century CE
Present-day Hungary	←	Magyars, ca. 896 CE

NORICUM
PANNONIA
DACIA
DALMATIA
ITALIA
MOESIA
THRACIA
MACEDONIA
ASIA

Enter the Magyars

A seminomadic group called the Magyars lived near the Ural Mountains and the Volga River, in what is Russia today. They lived among and were ruled by various Turkish groups. In the 800s, the Magyars began to rebel against their rulers.

There were several different Magyar tribes, and the Magyars decided they should have one leader. Headmen from each Magyar group gathered to drink a cup of blood, made of a mixture from each of them. After the ceremony, they chose a man named Árpád to be their military chieftain. Árpád is often considered the founder of Hungary.

The Magyars fought many small battles, and each time they were defeated, they were forced farther westward. Eventually, in about 896, the Magyars were driven over the Carpathian

Árpád (on horseback, left) was the leader of the most powerful Magyar tribe when he was chosen to lead all the Magyars.

Mountains toward the Danube and Tisza Rivers. The wide river basins were sparsely populated. The Magyars had learned to farm and raise livestock from the Turkish people, and rather than pursuing nomadic lives, they took advantage of the open, fertile landscape and settled into agricultural communities. The first Magyar settlements were on islands in the Danube River, south of where Budapest would later be.

Free of attacks from other groups, the Magyars expanded. Árpád led raids north into Germany and south into Italy, and the Magyars became powerful. But his military success did not last, and in 955 King Otto I of the Holy Roman Empire seized parts of western Transdanubia. Then, in 970, the eastern Roman Empire captured parts of Magyar holdings to the east.

The First King of Hungary

During the tenth century, the Roman Catholic religion was taking hold in the region. Árpád's great-great-grandson, Stephen (István in Hungarian), went to the pope, the leader of the Catholic Church, and asked to be crowned king of Hungary. The pope sent a jeweled crown to Stephen, and Stephen became the first king of Hungary on Christmas Day in the year 1000. By converting to Christianity, Hungary joined the community of Christian nations in Europe.

Stephen built churches, schools, and a massive monastery to house monks. He ordered everyone but priests to marry and have children. He also introduced new methods of farming. Stephen consolidated his rule over the country by granting large parcels of land to nobles (people of high rank)

and establishing a feudal system. In such a system, the nobles own the land, and the workers, called serfs, farm the land, raise livestock, and manage the household and grounds. In exchange, the feudal landowner protects the serfs from attackers. Stephen became widely respected throughout Europe.

Stephen being crowned king of Hungary. In 1083, the pope declared Stephen a saint, and Saint Stephen is today the patron saint of Hungary.

Fighting for Control

Stephen's heirs added to his achievements. They extended Hungarian rule over Slavic territories as well as Croatia. But one, Andrew II, damaged Stephen's legacy. Andrew was fond of luxuries and loved to associate with foreign nobles. He gave large land grants to foreign nobles, who in turn raised taxes on the serfs. Magyar landowners grew envious of the wealthier and more powerful foreigners. When Andrew II raised taxes, the Magyar people, serfs and nobles alike, rebelled. In 1222, Magyar nobles forced Andrew II to sign a document called the Golden Bull, which limited his power, created laws, and formed a parliament.

In 1240, Béla IV, Andrew II's son, sat on the throne while armies of the Mongols, an empire based in central Asia, terrorized eastern and central Europe. The Mongols fought with a secret weapon—gunpowder brought from China. When the Mongols swept into Hungary, the Magyar army was powerless against the Mongol weaponry. Hungary was devastated, and nearly half the population was killed. The Mongol ruler established his throne in Buda, but in 1242 he died and the Mongols left.

Following the departure of the Mongols, Béla IV returned to the Hungarian throne. He encouraged the growth of cities and improved farming and mining methods. He invited foreigners to immigrate to Hungary. Arts, crafts, and trade flourished. But Béla IV died without an heir. He was the last of Árpád's line, so Hungary's nobles allowed a succession of foreign kings to rule. They were the kings of England, Poland, Austria, and Luxembourg. Eventually, Hungarian nobles decided to name a Hungarian infant king, and appointed a regent to oversee his rule until the child was grown. The regent, named John (János) Hunyadi, was an accomplished army general. In 1458, it was not the infant who became king, but rather Hunyadi's son Matthias.

King Matthias is often called Hungary's most important monarch. Like his father, he was a gifted warrior. He expanded Hungary's borders by conquering parts of Bohemia, Austria, and

John Hunyadi made a name for himself as a military general. Because of this success, in 1446, he was chosen to lead Hungary.

Poland. He also supported the arts, education, and the humanities. He established a new university and reformed the legal system. His actions turned Hungary from a backward, feudal country into one of the greatest kingdoms in central Europe.

After Matthias died without heirs, Hungarians crowned a weak and easily influenced man to be king. The parliament

Queen Beatrice of Aragon

In the fifth century, Europe's Middle Ages began. This was a period filled with war, disease, poverty, and religious conflict. In the fifteenth century, Europe began to emerge from its decline, led by city-states in Italy. The period became known as the Renaissance (meaning "rebirth"), and it was notable for the flowering of the arts and scientific thought.

The woman who helped lead Hungary out of the Middle Ages was Beatrice of Aragon. Born in 1457, she was the daughter of King Ferdinand and Queen Isabella of Naples, Italy. The princess was well educated, fluent in several languages, and an enthusiastic supporter of the arts. She turned down many marriage proposals before she chose to wed King Matthias.

Beatrice shared her knowledge of art, music, and classical literature with Matthias. She brought talented artists, sculptors, and craftspeople to the Hungarian court and established her own personal library and much of the official court library. Beatrice advised her

husband on political matters, and historians have called their marriage a shared rule. Because of their efforts, the kingdom of Hungary was the first outside of Italy to experience the Renaissance.

ruled the country and limited the freedoms granted to serfs. After many workers' revolts, parliament imposed even harsher restrictions on the serfs. Conflicts made the country vulnerable to outsiders, and before long the Turkish army overran Hungary and carved it into three sections. Western Hungary came under the control of the Habsburg Empire, ruled by the Austrian king. Central Hungary was annexed to the Ottoman Empire. Turkish rulers established themselves in Buda and extracted as much wealth from the country as they could. The eastern region called Transylvania became an independent state.

Conflict and Peace

In the sixteenth century, religious conflict in Europe was rising. Many people were objecting to practices in the Roman Catholic Church. Some people claimed that the church's teachings were not rooted in the Bible, while others said the church was corrupt. People opposed to the Catholic Church became known as Protestants. Many Hungarians adopted the new Protestant faith, and by 1554, Transylvania was a Protestant state. Western Hungary's rulers, the Habsburgs, were Roman Catholic.

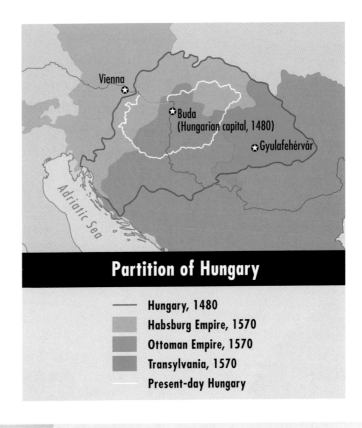

Partition of Hungary

- — Hungary, 1480
- Habsburg Empire, 1570
- Ottoman Empire, 1570
- Transylvania, 1570
- — Present-day Hungary

Protestant Hero

In the center of Budapest stands Heroes' Square, a large monument and plaza built in 1896 to celebrate one thousand years of Magyars in Hungary. The square honors many Magyar kings, soldiers, and revolutionaries. One statue portrays István Bocskay (left), a Transylvanian prince and follower of the Protestant leader John Calvin. Bocskay worked with the Ottoman Empire to fend off the Catholic Habsburgs of Austria. In 1606, he and the Austrian archduke Matthias signed the Treaty of Vienna granting religious freedom for Hungary's Protestant believers.

After many uprisings, the Transylvanians, with the support of the Ottoman army, attacked the Habsburgs. The Habsburgs enlisted other Catholic kingdoms to defeat the Ottomans.

After the Ottomans departed, Austria and Germany began to colonize Hungary. Still under Habsburg rule, Hungary nonetheless experienced new freedoms. The Habsburgs reinstated the power of the Magyar nobles and granted greater freedoms to the working people. Under the rule of the Austrian empress Maria Theresa, Hungary enjoyed a period of

An eighteenth-century view of Buda, which lay along the hilly western banks of the Danube

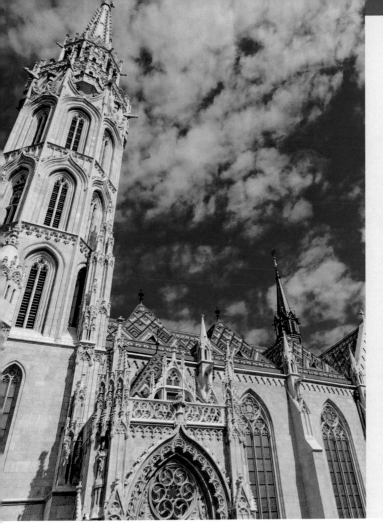

Matthias Church

King Matthias was married twice in the beautiful Gothic cathedral in Budapest that bears his name. The Austro-Hungarian Empire was created inside its majestic walls when Emperor Franz Josef and his wife, Elizabeth, were crowned.

The invading Mongols had originally constructed the building in the Middle Ages. After the Mongols left, Catholics made additions to the building, and for more than five hundred years, royal celebrations were held in the stately cathedral. In 1541, at the start of the Ottoman Turk conquest, the cathedral was converted into a Muslim mosque. The Christian carvings, sculptures, and paintings were removed, and the walls were painted white. The rows of benches were also removed and thick Turkish carpets were laid on the floor for the Muslim faithful to kneel on while they prayed. In 1699, Hungarians drove the Ottomans out of Buda, and the building was left in ruins. Again, Catholics reclaimed and rebuilt Matthias Church. Today, it towers over the city as a reminder of Hungary's turbulent past.

peace and prosperity. Cities, especially Buda and Pest, which would eventually combine to form Budapest, were rebuilt. A floating bridge was constructed across the Danube, connecting the two cities. Maria Theresa also did what she could to improve the standard of living for workers.

National Pride

In the beginning of the nineteenth century, Hungarian nobles sought a national identity. They wanted modernization

and independence from Austria. Count István Széchenyi, a Magyar noble, used his personal wealth to build railroads and the first permanent bridge across the Danube between Buda and Pest. He also donated his art collection to establish the Hungarian National Museum and founded the Hungarian Academy of Sciences.

By the mid-nineteenth century, many people in Europe were opposed to being ruled by nobles and kings. They hoped to replace the old monarchies with republics, where people voted for representatives who would govern. Several revolutions shook Europe, including one in Hungary.

In 1848, a journalist named Lajos Kossuth led the revolution. Kossuth and his supporters declared Hungary independent, and Kossuth became the president of the revolutionary government. But the revolt was soon crushed by the Austrian and Russian armies.

Austria, however, had ongoing disputes with other European powers and it did not want any more enemies. So in 1867, it signed a compromise agreement with Magyar nobles. Hungary was allowed to deal with its own internal affairs but joined together with Austria in foreign affairs. The alliance was known as the Austro-Hungarian Empire. The new Hungarian government promoted Magyar culture and established the Hungarian language as the official national language. Peace reigned for nearly a half century.

Leading a Revolution

As a young man, Lajos Kossuth was a lawyer and an outspoken member of parliament who urged Hungarians to rebel against Austria. He spent the years 1837 to 1840 jailed for his opinions. After his release, Kossuth worked as a journalist. Although he himself was from a noble family, he argued that nobles should have to pay taxes. He also maintained that peasants should be freed from many of the laws that limited what they could do, and that Hungarian should be made the official language of the entire country. Kossuth was appointed governor in 1849, during the Revolution of 1848. In this war between Austria and Hungary, Hungary nearly achieved independence, but Russia entered the war and Hungary was defeated. Kossuth went into exile. He is remembered for his bravery and patriotism and a statue of him stands in Heroes' Square in Budapest.

Archduke Franz Ferdinand and his wife, Sophie, Duchess of Hohenberg, were killed while driving through Sarajevo, now the capital of Bosnia and Herzegovina.

A Time of War

While it was somewhat calm in Hungary, tensions were rising in Europe. Germany, Austria-Hungary, and Italy formed a pact called the Triple Alliance to defend one another in the event of conflict. In response to a possible threat, France, Russia, and Britain did the same. On June 28, 1914, six Serbian rebels assassinated Archduke Franz Ferdinand, the heir to the Austro-Hungarian throne. The Triple Alliance blamed Serbia, and on July 28, Germany declared war on Serbia. Serbia was aligned with France, Russia, and Britain. The German army chose to attack France first, but as the army advanced, it invaded the neutral country of Belgium. Britain was outraged and declared war on Germany. The Ottoman Empire joined forces with the Triple Alliance. In August, Austria-Hungary declared war on France and Russia, while Britain declared war on Austria-Hungary.

The war, today known as World War I, ripped through Europe causing widespread destruction and taking more than ten million lives. Austria-Hungary sent about eight million troops into battle. More than one million of them were killed, and more than three and a half million soldiers and civilians from Austria-Hungary were wounded. Eventually, the Allies—France, Britain, Russia, the United States, and others—defeated the Triple Alliance and its supporters. On June 4, 1920, Hungary signed a peace treaty called the Treaty of Trianon.

The Treaty of Trianon included severe penalties for Hungary. The country was divided up, and much of its land was given to neighboring countries. At the start of the war, Hungary's area was 125,641 square miles (325,409 sq km). After the treaty, it was reduced to 35,893 square miles (92,962 sq km). Hungary's population dropped from nearly twenty-one million to less than eight million. Under the treaty, Hungary was also charged a financial penalty, and its army was limited to thirty-five thousand soldiers, whose sole responsibility was defending its borders and keeping peace within the country.

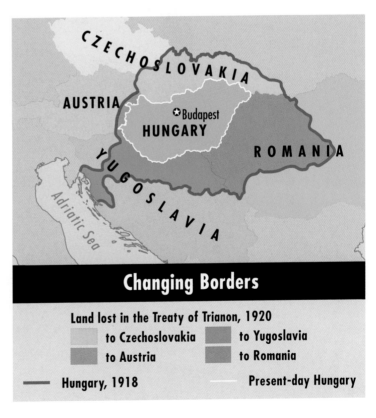

Changing Borders

Land lost in the Treaty of Trianon, 1920
- to Czechoslovakia
- to Austria
- to Yugoslavia
- to Romania
— Hungary, 1918   — Present-day Hungary

Changing Alliances

While World War I raged, Russian workers revolted against their government. They were communists who believed that workers would be better off if government controlled the land, manufacturing, transportation, education, and agriculture. In 1919, the Hungarian government was also taken over by communists.

Miklós Horthy, a Hungarian admiral, defeated the Hungarian communists and became regent of Hungary. Under his government, Hungary faced high unemployment

Miklós Horthy led Hungary from 1920 to 1944. Under his leadership, Hungary entered into an alliance with Nazi Germany.

and resentment between social classes. He appointed prime ministers who took voting rights away from the poor, gave the best jobs to friends and supporters, and bribed unions and other activists to go along with the government's policies. The government adopted many campaigns against opposition parties, non-Magyar ethnic groups, and especially Jewish citizens.

In the 1930s, Adolf Hitler became the leader of Germany and promoted aggressive nationalism. Fearing communism, Hitler signed a pact with Japan and Italy to counter the threat of communism coming from China and the Soviet Union, a large country that had been created when Russia joined together with neighboring lands. Before the war, Hungary became allied with Germany because of their shared anticommunist stance and because it hoped to regain some of the territory it had lost in the Treaty of Trianon. In 1938, negotiations between Germany, Hungary, and other countries led to some of Hungary's territory being returned in what is known as the First Vienna Award. More territory was returned to Hungary in 1940, in what is called the Second Vienna Award.

By this time, World War II had already started. In 1939, Germany had annexed Austria and invaded Poland. France and Britain then declared war on Germany. Germany swiftly took over much of western Europe. In Germany and elsewhere in Europe, Jewish people were being heavily persecuted. Hitler's Nazi Party robbed them of their belongings and forced them to live in crowded ghettos, and put them to work in labor camps. Ultimately, Hitler's Nazi regime captured millions of European Jews and forced them into concentration

Over the course of two months in 1944, more than 430,000 Hungarian Jews were sent to the Auschwitz concentration camp in Poland. Most of them died there.

camps where most were worked to death or murdered. People from other groups that were considered undesirable, such as the Roma, were also put into concentration camps and killed.

Germany was opposed by countries known as the Allies, which included Britain, France, the Soviet Union, and the United States. Hungarian leaders feared the communist threat posed by the Soviet Union. During the war, Hungarian and German soldiers battled the Soviet Union, and Hungary suffered huge losses. In 1944, Germany was concerned that Hungary would back out of the Triple Alliance, so Nazi generals ordered German troops to invade Hungary. The Nazis suppressed all Hungarian opposition, suspended civil rights, and created a police state. More than 500,000 Hungarian Jews, as well as many Roma, died at the hands of the Nazis during the war. However, many Hungarian citizens risked their own safety in helping more than 250,000 Hungarian Jews survive.

Under Communism

The Soviet Union defeated Germany's troops in Hungary in 1945. Germany withdrew, leaving Hungary under the control of the Soviet Union. In 1948, the communists rigged the elections. Hungary became a communist nation and was renamed the Hungarian People's Republic. Hungarian workers were forced to work on government-owned collective farms and were

People fill the streets of Budapest in 1948 to celebrate the merger of the Hungarian Communist Party and the Social Democratic Party, forming the Hungarian Workers' Party. Although other parties were still officially allowed at the time, they had no power.

paid far less than before. The state also took over other work-places, including factories, shops, and restaurants. Religious leaders led the resistance to communist rule, but religion was strongly discouraged under communism. Some church buildings were taken over, and priests imprisoned.

On October 23, 1956, anti-Soviet protesters gathered in Budapest. They demanded better pay and working conditions, and condemned the military presence. Demonstrations spread around the country, leading the communist government to make some compromises. They appointed a reformer named

Hungarian farmers work together on a collective farm, on fields they once owned individually.

Imre Nagy as prime minister. Nagy abolished the state security police and one-party communist rule and called for free elections. On November 1, he announced that Hungary would become a neutral country and would withdraw from the Warsaw Pact, an alliance agreement signed by communist countries. Anticommunist demonstrators took to the streets. One group captured a Soviet tank, and another toppled a large statue of the Soviet leader Joseph Stalin. On November 4, Soviet troops invaded Hungary and crushed the revolution. More than three thousand people were killed. Imre Nagy was later executed.

Although some of Hungary's new leaders attempted reforms, the communist party was still part of the government. But the new government lifted bans on free speech laws and reduced censorship, and gradually practices changed. In 1968, some private

During the 1956 uprising, Hungarian protesters in Budapest tipped over a statue of Soviet leader Joseph Stalin.

ownership of farms and businesses began to be allowed. In time, workers, educators, and trade unions formed political parties.

Modern Times

In the autumn of 1989, the world watched as stunning changes happened in the Soviet Union and other communist countries. In Hungary, barbed wire fences along the borders were removed. People chanted in the streets of Budapest, and many communist government officials resigned. Hungary declared itself a democratic republic. Free elections were held in May 1990, and a coalition of several different parties came to power.

In 2004, Hungary was accepted into the European Union (EU), a powerful organization made up of most European countries. By eliminating taxes on goods shipped between the EU member countries, the organization had created one large market in Europe, which made many goods cheaper. The EU also allowed people to travel freely between the member nations, and in many cases allowed people from one EU nation to work in other EU nations. Membership in the EU helped boost Hungary's standard of living.

In 2015, a massive migrant crisis strained Hungary's relationship with other EU countries. Hundreds of thousands of refugees from Syria and other war-torn nations in the Middle East and Africa poured across Hungary's borders with Serbia and Croatia. The migrants wanted to move on to Germany or other wealthy countries. Germany, however, wanted the refugees spread out throughout all of the EU member nations.

Poorer nations such as Hungary, however, argued that they did not have the resources to care for the newcomers. As the flow of migrants continued, more extreme measures were taken. Hungary built a barbed wire fence along its border with Serbia, where many migrants were entering. Meanwhile, some European countries reestablished passport controls at their borders so that people could no longer travel freely between the EU member states. Throughout the crisis, Hungary's government seemed intent on asserting its independence.

Refugees from the Middle East and Africa walk from the train station in Hegyeshalom, Hungary, toward the Austrian border.

CHAPTER 5

Ruling Hungary

HUNGARY WAS ONE OF THE FIRST COUNTRIES IN Europe to establish a constitutional form of government. On March 21, 1919, after the fall of the Austro-Hungarian Empire and the end of World War I, Hungary called for a government made up of many political parties. But in 1944, Hungary was taken over by Nazi Germany, and in 1945 by the Soviet Union. The leaders these foreign powers put in place did not follow the Hungarian constitution. In 1949, a communist constitution was drawn up, based on the Soviet constitution of 1936. That model included lawmaking by decree rather than by elected officials. The Communist Party was the only party with power. Freedom of speech, the press, religion, and the right to assemble were limited.

Opposite: **The Hungarian parliament building was constructed in the late nineteenth and early twentieth centuries, in the years after Buda and Pest merged to form the city of Budapest.**

Hungary's Flag

Hungary's flag consists of three equal horizontal bands of red, white, and green. The design of the flag was inspired by the French revolutionary flag. The colors have been used in Hungary's coat of arms since the Middle Ages. Some people say red stands for strength, white for faithfulness, and green for hope. Others suggest that the red stands for the blood spilled in defense of the land, white represents freedom, and green symbolizes the fertile soil.

Constitutional Changes

In 1989, the Soviet Union withdrew from Hungary, and Hungary soon drafted an amended constitution that created a legislature capable of controlling the executive branch of government, allowed a multiparty system, and established a court to review what laws were legal under the constitution.

In 2012, conservative Hungarian leaders amended the nation's constitution once again. The amended constitution called Hungary a Christian nation and incorporated some conservative Christian ideas into it, such as opposing same-sex marriage. The constitution also made changes to the judicial system. Objections to these changes came from within Hungary and from the EU. For example, many people believed the changes to the court system undermined the independence of the judicial branch of government. Because of the outcry, Hungarian leaders made additional changes to the constitution in 2013, which helped calm some of the concerns.

Hungary's constitution divides its government into three branches: executive, legislative, and judicial. Hungary's government is a parliamentary democracy. Most of the power of a parliamentary democracy lies with the legislative branch.

Executive Branch

The executive branch is made up of a president, who acts as head of state, and a prime minister, who is the head of government. The parliament, known as the National Assembly, elects the president to a five-year term. A largely ceremonial role, the president acts as commander in chief of the armed forces, signs bills into law, and is involved in international relations. He or she can also declare a state of emergency.

Viktor Orbán served as prime minister from 1998 to 2002 and again beginning in 2010. He has been called an authoritarian figure because he has limited freedom of the press and the power of opposition political parties.

The Castle City

Budapest, the capital of Hungary, has a long history. In the fifth century, Roman conquerors built forts in a city they called Aquincum, which later became known as Óbuda (Old Buda). Later, Mongol invaders built a castle on a hill overlooking the Danube and the city of Buda, which had grown just to the south of the old settlement. In the fourteenth century, Buda became Hungary's capital city, and the city across the Danube, Pest, was the center of trade. On November 17, 1873, the three cities: Buda, Pest, and Óbuda were united into one.

With its ancient buildings, stunning architecture, and location on the banks of the Danube River, Budapest is considered one of the most beautiful cities in Europe. Buda Castle was home to many of Hungary's royal families. It has been added onto, destroyed, rebuilt, attacked, and added onto again. As a result, it has a wide variety of architectural styles. Next to the castle are museums, galleries, and a cathedral. In Pest, along the banks of the Danube, stands the lavish Gothic-inspired parliament building, built between 1885 and 1902.

Budapest is by far the country's largest city with a population of 1,744,665. A large majority of the population is ethnic Hungarian (Magyar). Many other people in Budapest are of Roma, Romanian, German, and Slav descent.

Budapest

(Map labels: National Sports Pool, Margaret Island, RÓZSADOMB, ÚJLIPÓTVÁROS, Budapest Zoo and Botanical Garden, Gundel, Széchenyi Baths, ZUGLÓ, Museum of Fine Arts, Heroes' Square, Vajdahunyad Castle, Budapest City Park, Canadian Embassy, Nyugati Train Station, TERÉZVÁROS, VÍZIVÁROS, Parliament Building, Danube River, Postal Savings Bank, ERZSÉBETVÁROS, Franz Liszt Academy of Music, ISTVÁNMEZŐ, Puskás Ferenc Stadium, Matthias Church, U.S. Embassy, Hungarian State Opera House, Keleti Train Station, László Papp Sports Arena, Vérmező, Hungarian Academy of Sciences, St. Stephen's Basilica, Hungarian Jewish Museum, Great Synagogue, PEST, Kerepesi Cemetery, Buda Castle (Hungarian National Gallery, National Széchényi Library of Hungary, Budapest History Museum, Museum of Contemporary Art), Hungarian National Museum, BUDA, Citadella, JÓZSEFVÁROS, Central Market Hall, Bálna Budapest, Orczy Park, Gellért Baths, Hungarian Natural History Museum, St. Stephen Hospital, TISZTVISELŐTELEP, LÁGYMÁNYOS, Planetarium, Budapest Technical University, Saint László Hospital, Groupama Arena, Palace of Arts; scale: 0 1 mile, 0 1 kilometer)

The prime minister is voted on by the members of the legislature. The prime minister is the most powerful member of the executive branch. He or she appoints cabinet ministers of government departments, such as education or agriculture. The prime minister's tasks include guiding government policy, overseeing cabinet meetings, representing government to the people, and ensuring that government decisions are followed. The prime minister is elected for a four-year term.

The National Assembly

The National Assembly is a unicameral legislature, meaning that it only has one lawmaking body, unlike the United States, which has two, the Senate and House of Representatives. Hungary's election process is more complicated than most. Citizens are given two ballots. One ballot is to elect a single mandate candidate, meaning an individual representative from a district, who will represent that district in parliament. The other ballot is used to vote on national lists of people belonging to various political parties. When the voting is complete, political party officials choose the members of parliament from these national lists.

Each member of the National Assembly is elected to a four-year term. There are 199 members of parliament—106 single mandate members and 93 members selected from national lists. Generally, only four to six parties win a seat in parliament. The largest party in recent years has been a conservative party called Fidesz. Other significant parties include the Hungarian Socialist Party and Jobbik, a nationalist party.

The National Assembly enacts new laws and amends former laws. The legislature also elects the president, prime minister, the president of Hungary's highest court, constitutional court judges, and many high-level commissioners. The National Assembly may also participate in decisions about military actions, declare war, or sign a peace treaty. It may also remove a prime minister through a vote called a "vote of no confidence." If the parliament is unable to function in its assigned roles, the president may dissolve parliament and call for new elections. The National Assembly may also

Members of the National Assembly gather for a session in 2014.

National Anthem

Ferenc Kölcsey wrote the words to the national anthem in 1823, and Ferenc Erkel set them to music. The song, called simply "Himnusz" ("Hymn") was adopted as the national anthem in 1844.

Hungarian lyrics

Isten, áldd meg a magyart
Jó kedvvel, bőséggel,
Nyújts feléje védő kart,
Ha küzd ellenséggel;
Bal sors akit régen tép,
Hozz rá víg esztendőt,
Megbűnhődte már e nép
A múltat s jövendőt!

English translation

O Lord, bless the nation of Hungary
With your grace and bounty
Extend toward it your guarding arm
During strife with its enemies
Long torn by ill fate
Bring upon it a time of relief
This nation has suffered for all sins
Of the past and of the future!

Judges preside over a trial in Budapest.

dissolve itself. The most recent constitution states that any issue before the parliament must be approved by a two-thirds majority vote.

Judicial Branch

The highest court in Hungary is called the Curia. It has three departments: criminal, civil, and administrative. The court is responsible for examining appeals of other courts, reviewing decisions, and interpreting the law for lower courts to follow. The Curia has a president of the court, elected by the prime minister, and two vice presidents. Hungary also has five regional courts of appeal, which review cases tried in lower courts. Criminal and civil cases are heard in twenty regional courts. They also review decisions made by smaller district courts.

Hungary also has a special court known as the constitutional court. This court reviews cases that require the constitution to be interpreted. The president of the Curia can request the constitutional court to review a case or law. However, the constitutional court cannot overturn any law that was passed by a two-thirds majority of the National Assembly.

Hungary's National Government

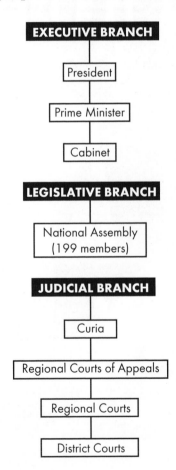

EXECUTIVE BRANCH

President

Prime Minister

Cabinet

LEGISLATIVE BRANCH

National Assembly
(199 members)

JUDICIAL BRANCH

Curia

Regional Courts of Appeals

Regional Courts

District Courts

CHAPTER 6

On the Rebound

HUNGARIANS ARE EXCEPTIONALLY ADAPTABLE. Through the many twists and turns of their history, they have worked tirelessly, growing their own food and providing vital goods for one another. From prosperous times to painful downturns, Hungarian workers have earned their livelihoods through cleverness and determination.

Putting Food on the Table

Since prehistoric times, Hungarian farmers have benefited from the fertile soil of their vast plains. Until the twentieth century, agriculture was the leading source of income for the nation. Although manufacturing, trade, and services provide more jobs today, Hungary's farmers produce nearly all the food Hungarians consume. The nation's crops include grains, such as wheat, corn, and rice; fruit and vegetables, such as apples, potatoes, and soybeans; and other crops such as sugar beets, sunflowers (grown for seed oil), and nuts, such as walnuts and almonds; and spices, such as ginger and Hungarian paprika pepper. Hungary is also famous for growing grapes for wine, in particular a special sweet wine grape called Tokay.

Hungarian ranchers raise sheep, goats, beef cattle, dairy cows, hogs, and chickens. Fish is also raised in Hungary. As far back as the sixteenth century, Hungarians raised fish in ponds and wetlands. When people began eating more meat, fish farming, called aquaculture, declined. However, fish farms came back into favor in the early twentieth century, when

Hungarian workers collect fish from a net at a fish farm. In Hungary, fish is eaten most often on holidays.

people were struggling to make ends meet and raising livestock was more expensive than raising fish. Today, Hungary aquaculture produces more than 15,000 tons of fish each year.

Natural Resources

Hungarians have long benefited from their natural resources of timber, natural gas, oil, coal, and minerals. Hungary, once heavily forested, now has declining forest reserves because of logging. However, at the urging of environmentalists, Hungary has replanted forests. From 2000 to 2010, Hungary replanted 600,000 acres (200,000 ha) of forest. In 2013, Hungary produced more than 200 million cubic feet (6 million cu m) of timber for construction materials, papermaking, and firewood.

During the Soviet era in Hungary, there was a focus on mining, especially iron ore. Mining is not a major industry today, except for coal and bauxite, an aluminum ore. Hungary has one of the richest supplies of bauxite in Europe, which is essential for making concrete. Other minerals mined in Hungary are copper, zinc, mercury, and uranium.

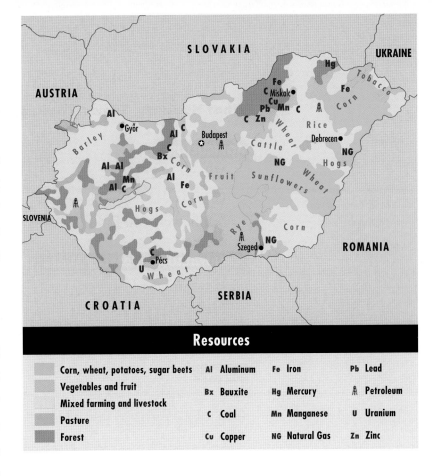

Resources

Corn, wheat, potatoes, sugar beets	Al Aluminum Fe Iron Pb Lead
Vegetables and fruit	Bx Bauxite Hg Mercury Petroleum
Mixed farming and livestock	C Coal Mn Manganese U Uranium
Pasture	Cu Copper NG Natural Gas Zn Zinc
Forest	

What Hungary Grows, Makes, and Mines

AGRICULTURE

Wheat (2013)	5 million metric tons
Corn (2013)	4.5 million metric tons
Sunflower seed for oil (2014)	1.3 million metric tons

MANUFACTURING (VALUE ADDED)

Electronics (2008)	US$34,000,000,000
Medicines (2013)	US$1,800,000,000
Automobiles (2013)	227,000 vehicles

MINING

Coal (2012)	10,000,000 metric tons
Bauxite (2012)	255,000 metric tons

Energy

Hungary has supplies of coal, oil, and natural gas. Coal once produced nearly half of Hungary's energy needs, but it now provides less than one-third. Because coal-burning electric power plants pollute the air, Hungary has either closed them or improved technology in them over the past decade. Oil and natural gas were discovered in the 1930s. Today, a combination of natural gas, nuclear power, and coal supply about one-half of the country's energy needs, and much of the rest comes from oil, mainly imported from Russia. Hungary is making strides in using renewable energy—power from water, wind, and the sun.

Manufacturing

Manufacturing is the most important industry in Hungary. More than one-quarter of the economy relies on income from manufacturing. When the Soviet Union controlled Hungary's economy, it emphasized heavy industry, such as the production of steel, chemicals, and machines. By the 1990s, those factories were outmoded. Forward-thinking business-people have since introduced new technologies that are more energy efficient, profitable, and better for the environment. Today, manufacturing is much improved. Some of the major manufacturing operations include medicines and medical instruments, food processing, electronics and electronic parts, and automobiles. Recently, German automakers Audi and Mercedes-Benz have built large factories in Hungary, giving hundreds of workers new, well-paying jobs.

The number of cars manufactured in Hungary has been growing steadily since the late 1990s.

About two-thirds of Hungary's workers are employed in service industries.

Services

Service industries are also vital to Hungary's economy. Services are jobs people perform for one another, such as those employed in health care, banking, insurance, education, law, retail, government, and police and fire departments. Tourism is a growing industry, employing tens of thousands of people in hotels, restaurants, and tour companies. Hungary is one of the top twenty most-visited countries. Tourists come to enjoy historic architecture, museums, prehistoric artifacts, and more. Nature lovers enjoy exploring national parks filled with caves, rivers, thermal springs, lakes, and wildlife.

Trade is a major part of Hungary's economy. Because Hungary is centrally located between Europe and Asia, many companies build or store their goods in Hungary for easy transport between countries.

From 1949 to 1991, most of Hungary's trade was with the Soviet Union and communist countries in central and eastern Europe. The countries often bartered for goods or sold them to each other below cost. The Soviet Union made up the difference in cost, so when Hungary became independent, it no longer had the benefit of lower prices. Its economy declined swiftly, and the cost of basic goods skyrocketed. The country was forced to take out large loans from European banks in order to keep its economy afloat. Gradually, Hungary improved its production and exported more goods to Russia and elsewhere in Europe and Asia.

When Hungary became a member of the EU, Germany became Hungary's biggest trading partner. Hungary also exports large amounts of goods to Romania, Slovakia, and Austria. After Germany, Hungary's biggest import partners are Russia, China, and Austria.

Money Facts

The currency of Hungary is called the forint. In the fourteenth century, Hungary used gold coins called forints, which came from Florence, Italy. The coins are no longer in use, but the name remains. Coins come in values of 5, 10, 20, 50, 100, and 200 forints, while paper banknotes have values of 500, 1,000, 2,000, 5,000, 10,000, and 20,000 forints.

The latest 500-forint note has a portrait of the Transylvanian prince Rákóczi, who led an uprising against the Habsburgs in the 1700s. On the back of the bill is an image of the Castle of Sárospatak, a medieval castle in eastern Hungary. In 2015, US$1.00 equaled 281 forints. Euros, the currency of the EU, are also accepted in Hungary.

Transportation and Communications

Hungary is a major European transportation hub. There are nearly 5,000 miles (8,000 km) of railroad tracks, 200,000 miles (320,000 km) of roads, and 1,000 miles (1,600 km) of navigable rivers. Barges carrying goods on the Danube connect with trains that can bring goods from seaports in the Mediterranean Sea to the North Sea.

Crowded Budapest has a modern public transportation system, making it easy for residents and visitors to move about the city on buses, subways, trolleys, and bicycles. The city is

Budapest has a complex public transportation system, which includes trams, buses, subways, and trains.

truly the nation's center—all major roads begin in Budapest and extend outward.

During the Soviet era, there were few television and radio stations, or publishing companies. After independence, many new media companies emerged. However, as is the case worldwide, more media has shifted to the Internet and mobile telecommunication networks. More than eleven million cell phones are in use in Hungary. Seven million Hungarians use the Internet, and more than four million Hungarians have joined Facebook.

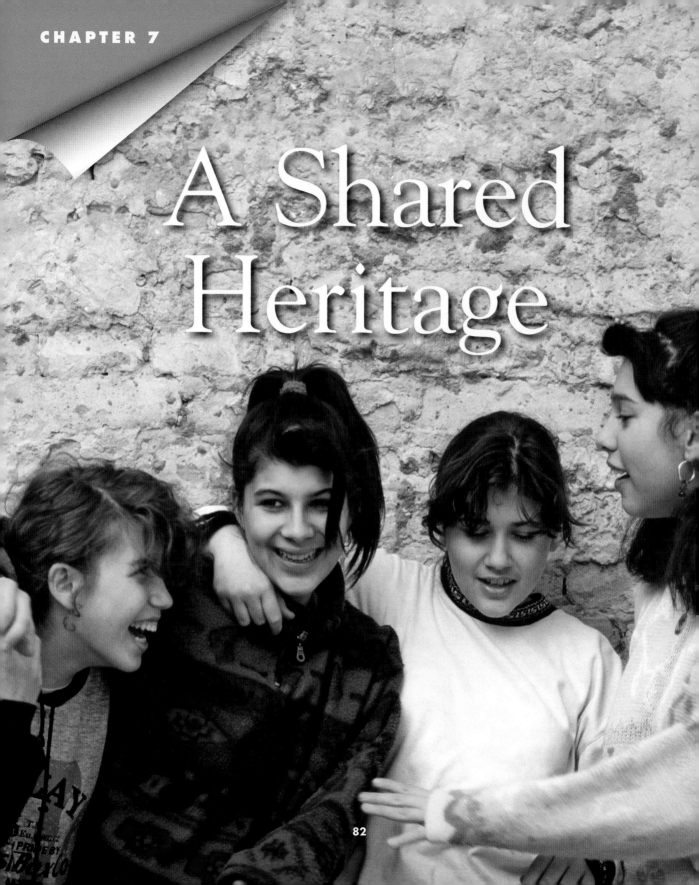

CHAPTER 7

A Shared Heritage

N THE NINTH CENTURY, LARGE GROUPS OF MAGYAR people arrived in Hungary and settled much of the land, creating a powerful culture and speaking a unique language. Among Europeans, Hungarians are the largest group of people to speak a language whose roots are Asian. There are about 12 million Hungarian speakers in the world, and nearly all live in Hungary. Hungarian is the country's official language and it is also one of the official languages of the European Union.

Opposite: **About one-quarter of Hungarians are under age twenty-five.**

The Magyars

The Ural Mountains, the original home of the Magyars, lie on the continent of Asia. After seven Magyar tribes, two Turkic tribes, and one other small group settled in Hungary, Mongol armies attacked their settlements. The tribes joined forces. Many historians agree that the name *Hungary* likely comes from the union of these ten tribes, because *onorgur* means "ten arrows" in the Turkish language.

Languages Spoken by Hungarians	
Hungarian	99.6%
English	16%
German	11.2%
Russian	1.6%
Romanian	1.3%
French	1.2%
Other	4.2%

The Magyars were the first and largest group of people to permanently inhabit Hungary. Over the centuries, their culture and traditions spread to every corner of the nation. Nearly all place-names and personal names come from the Hungarian language. Many newcomers change their names to Hungarian names after they arrive.

Ethnic Hungary

There are thirteen ethnic or national minorities in Hungary. The largest groups are the Roma and the Germans. Additionally, Jewish people, a religious minority, have long lived in Hungary.

Magyars in Budapest in the 1800s

Many ethnic or national minorities came to Hungary to farm, while others came as refugees, including groups of Romanians and Serbs. Also, Hungary's borders changed many times, and when this happened, some people found themselves living on land that had become a part of Hungary. Newcomers often settled near one another in rural communities, staying with their own ethnic groups. But most learned to speak Hungarian. The rights of minorities are clearly spelled out in the constitution, and the government of Hungary supports education and special programs to help minority communities keep their national or ethnic heritage alive.

Until the twentieth century, Jewish people were one of the largest non-Magyar groups in Hungary. Most lived in cities, especially Budapest. They built Jewish schools, businesses, museums, libraries, and houses of worship. Many worked in journalism,

Ethnic Serbs perform a folk dance in Deszk, in southern Hungary. Most ethnic Serbs in Hungary live in the south.

Workers prepare dishes at a Roma restaurant in Budapest. Social aid groups worked to open the restaurant in 2012 to help inform other Hungarians and foreign tourists about Roma culture.

medicine, business, and education. At one point, Hungarian Jews formed the third-largest Jewish community in Europe. But the Nazis killed half a million Hungarian Jews during World War II. Today, Hungarian Jews are rebuilding schools, businesses, and public buildings to preserve their ancient culture.

The Roma

The Roma, sometimes called Romani, are the descendants of people who fled persecution in their homeland in northern India more than 1,500 years ago. They first arrived in Europe during the Middle Ages. The Europeans called them Gypsies. Europeans feared the Roma people because of their unfamiliar look—they were dark-skinned—and because they kept to themselves. The Roma people made a living traveling about, often in horse-drawn wagons, and plied their traditional trades such as metalworking, woodcarving, and basket making. In the eighteenth century, Empress Maria Theresa of Austria banned the name *Gypsy*, which was viewed negatively, but ordered the Roma to have fewer children. The government took Roma children away from their families so that they might be raised as "new Hungarians." By the twentieth century, most Roma had adopted the Hungarian language. In World War II, the Roma, like the Jews, were sent to death camps. More than sixty thousand Hungarian Roma people were killed. The Roma called it the Devouring.

Roma communities exist in most of the cities and towns in Hungary. Roma families tend to be large and close knit, and friends within the Roma community are very loyal to one another. Many Roma work in traditional occupations such as furniture making, guitar making, and recycling, but they also have become more involved in local government and community services. During the communist period in Hungary, many Roma were employed in large factories or mines, because Hungary's communist government required everyone to have a job. After the end of communism, Roma employees were usually fired before people from other ethnic groups. Many Roma are poor and outcast. Roma families might not send their

Ethnic Background (2011)

Hungarian	98.0%
Roma	3.6%
German	1.6%
Other	1.9%
No answer	14.7%

*Does not add up to 100% because people could give more than one answer.

children to public school since those schools do not treat their children equally. The government of Hungary and the EU are working to improve the standard of living for Roma people.

Speaking and Writing

Hungary has a high literacy rate. Nearly 99 percent of the population over age fifteen can read and write. Many Europeans consider Hungarian a difficult language to learn, so most Hungarian schoolchildren learn a second language, usually German or English. English has become the more popular second language among young adults who want to study abroad or pursue careers in business, science, and technology.

The Hungarian language belongs to a group of languages from northeastern Russia, called Finno-Ugric. The Finnish and Estonian languages are distant cousins of the Hungarian language. Hungarian uses fourteen vowels including *a*, *e*, *i*, *o*, and *u* with various accent marks. It also has nine grouped-consonant sounds, including *dzs*, which is pronounced something like the *dg* in "bridge." Nearly every letter in a word is pronounced.

The earliest activities of the Magyar people were recorded with the written word. They used runic script (ancient symbols and letters) and carved their legends into stone, wood, clay, and leather. But King Stephen demanded that all the runic writings be destroyed, and he ordered people to speak and write in Latin, the language of the Roman Catholic Church. Although Hungarian continued to be spoken, Latin was the official language of academics and government in Hungary until 1844.

Coming and Going

Generally, few people immigrate into Hungary because of its relatively poor economic conditions. In 2015, many thousands of refugees arrived in Hungary from Syria and other troubled regions, but most planned to pass through Hungary to other parts of Europe.

Many more people emigrate out of Hungary. In the late nineteenth and early twentieth centuries, thousands of impoverished Hungarians moved to the United States in hopes of

The first book printed in Hungary was produced in 1473. The Hungarian language Bible shown above dates from 1608.

making a better life for themselves. The largest numbers of them ended up in Ohio and New York. After World War II, many more people—most of them Jewish—left Hungary for the United States.

In the nineteenth and twentieth centuries, Hungarians immigrated to both the United States and Canada. This Hungarian meat shop is in Montreal, Canada.

Hungarian Wisdom

The Hungarian language is filled with sayings, or proverbs. Here are a few.

"Minden csoda három napig tart."

Translation: "Every miracle lasts only three days."
Meaning: What is new and exciting will wear off.

"Egyem meg a szivedet."

Translation: "I'd like to eat your heart."
Meaning: I love you (said to children with affection).

"A messzirol jött ember azt mond amit akar."

Translation: "The man who comes from afar says what he will."
Meaning: Beware of strangers.

"Nem akarásnak nyögés a vége."

Translation: "Moaning is the end for those who aren't willing (to work)."
Meaning: If you do not work hard, life will be difficult.

"Nem mind arany ami fénylik."

Translation: "Not everything that is shiny is gold."
Meaning: Things that are appealing may not always be good.

"Ki a kicsit nem becsüli, a nagyot nem érdemli."

Translation: "If you don't cherish the little, you don't deserve the big."
Meaning: Be grateful for the small things in life.

The population in Hungary has been declining since 2001. Two main groups are leaving—professionals and young adults. Many young people cannot find jobs and are tired of living with their parents. Some young people choose to go abroad to study, and many do not return. By being a part of the EU, Hungarian citizens can move around Europe freely, making migration easier. Well-educated young adults and professionals often have large college loans to repay. Many move to England or Germany, where jobs are more plentiful and wages are higher.

City and Town

Nearly two-thirds of the population of Hungary lives in cities, mainly Budapest and the surrounding area. Budapest is home to major universities, libraries, government offices, and international businesses, as well as cultural sites such as theaters, music halls, restaurants, and museums. It is also the heart of the tourist industry.

Besides Budapest, regional cities such as Debrecen, Pécs, and Győr act as agricultural, industrial, cultural, and commer-

Bükk National Park, located in the mountains of northern Hungary, is the nation's largest national park.

cial centers. As tourism increases, new cities are taking shape near national parks, thermal springs, and historic landmarks.

Housing is a major concern in many of Hungary's cities. The price of buying or renting a home is high and getting higher. A worldwide economic recession that started in 2008 left many Hungarians unable to keep their homes. Many who cannot afford to live in the city commute long distances to get to work or school.

Apart from Budapest and these few other cities, Hungary is very rural. Even in suburbs, neighborhoods feel like villages, with small homes nestled near parks and markets. Many Hungarians have gardens and grow much of their own food. Most people who live in small towns and villages work in agriculture or livestock rearing, and in some areas people work in mining. But people who live in towns and cities stay in close touch with the countryside. Many make weekend or vacation excursions to lakes, mountains, and parks, and many others frequently visit friends and family in the country on weekends and especially holidays.

Population of Major Cities (2014 est.)	
Budapest	1,744,665
Debrecen	203,914
Szeged	161,921
Miskolc	161,265
Pécs	146,581

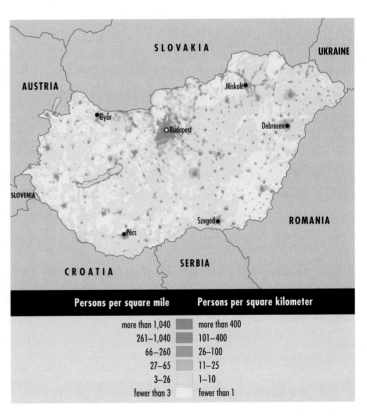

Persons per square mile	Persons per square kilometer
more than 1,040	more than 400
261–1,040	101–400
66–260	26–100
27–65	11–25
3–26	1–10
fewer than 3	fewer than 1

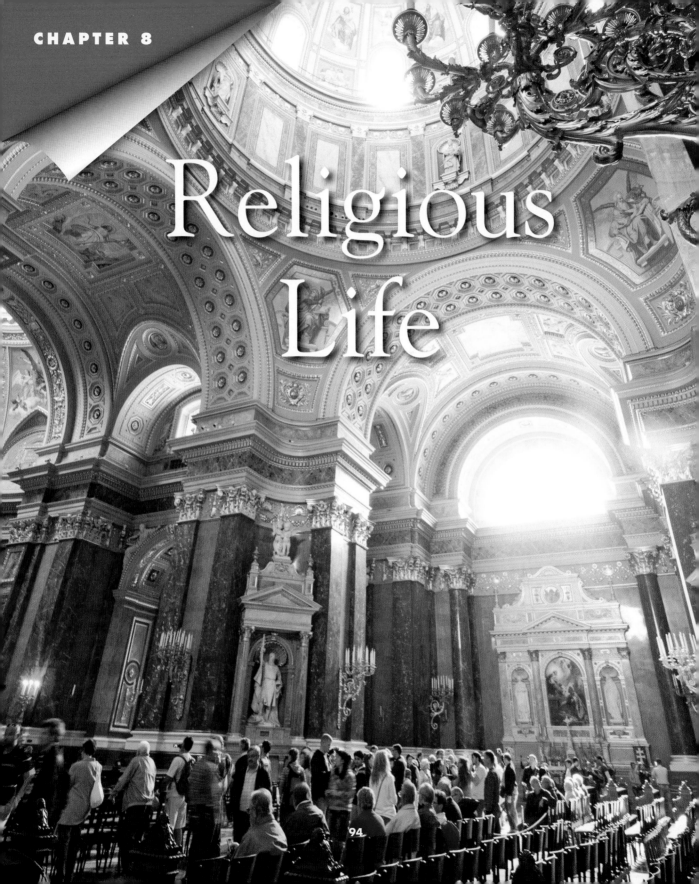

CHAPTER 8

Religious Life

"**G**OD BLESS THE HUNGARIANS!" SO STATES THE first line of Hungary's newest constitution. Christianity has been dominant in Hungary since King Stephen was crowned in 1000. The Hungarian constitution guarantees freedom of religion. The separation of church and state there is less strict than in the United States. In fact, in recent years, many publicly funded schools have been handed over to churches, and students at these schools are required to take part in religious services.

Opposite: **St. Stephen's Basilica, the largest Catholic church in Budapest, was completed in 1905.**

Christianity Through the Centuries

The early Magyars were pagan people who believed in several gods. In the ninth century, the Magyars stormed through central and eastern Europe. Finally, King Otto of the Holy Roman Empire defeated the Magyars. To make peace with King Otto, Géza, the Magyar chieftain, allowed Roman Catholic missionaries into Hungary. The missionaries began converting the Magyars to Catholicism, including Géza's son, who changed his name from Vajk to István (Stephen) when

Religion in Hungary (2011)	
Roman Catholic	37.1%
Reformed	11.6%
Lutheran	2.2%
Greek Catholic	1.8%
Other	1.9%
Nonreligious	16.7%
Atheist	1.5%
Undeclared	27.2%

A service is held in the Pannonhalma Abbey. Founded in 996, it is one of the oldest buildings in Hungary.

he was baptized. King Stephen and his Catholic wife forced their subjects to accept Christianity, through violence if no other means worked. Stephen formed alliances with neighboring Catholic countries. A group of Hungarians rebelled, but with the help of armies from other Catholic countries, they were defeated. Grateful, Stephen built an immense monastery called Pannonhalma Abbey near Győr and invited monks from Germany, France, and Italy to come to Hungary. They established schools and built churches.

In the 1500s, a movement known as the Reformation took hold in Europe. Scholars such as Martin Luther in Germany and John Calvin in France protested that the Catholic Church had too much power and too much money. The reformers were called Protestants, and many Hungarians converted to Protestantism. In the seventeenth century, the pope and the Habsburgs of Catholic Austria launched an attack on the reformers in what is known as the Counter-Reformation. The Habsburgs pressured Hungarians under their rule to return to Catholicism. Protestantism remained strong in the eastern parts of the country.

After World War II, the new communist government began sweeping land reforms, which included taking away property owned by churches and religious schools. Religious organizations, newspapers, and parishes were dissolved. More than 2,500 monks and nuns were deported.

After the Soviet troops left, the Hungarian government passed a law called the Freedom of Conscience and Religion,

The Great Reformed Church in Debrecen is the largest Protestant church in Hungary.

and returned property that had been taken from religious groups. Religious schools and hospitals reopened.

Christianity Today

Today, Roman Catholicism is Hungary's largest religious group. More than one out of every three Hungarians is Roman Catholic. The Catholic Church has thousands of places of worship in Hungary. This includes twenty major cathedrals and an ancient monastery.

Followers of the teachings of John Calvin belong to what is called the Reformed Church. John Calvin taught his followers that they cannot change their destiny and they must carefully obey the Bible's laws. The Reformed Church is the second-largest religious group in Hungary. Most of its mem-

The Biggest Church

The biggest building in Hungary and one of the largest cathedrals in Europe is the Esztergom Basilica, which sits along the Danube River in the little town of Esztergom. It is the seat of the Archbishop of Hungary, the most important Catholic official in the nation. The cathedral was first built in the tenth century, but it was attacked and rebuilt several times, so it is now a mixture of architectural styles. Inside there are high ceilings, massive altars, and the largest painting in the world done on a single piece of canvas. The painting of Mary, the mother of Jesus Christ, ascending into heaven, was completed in the 1800s. It is 44 feet (13.4 m) tall—as tall as a four-story building—and 22 feet (6.7 m) wide.

bers live in the eastern part of the country, near Debrecen.

The followers of Martin Luther belong to the church known as the Evangelical-Lutheran Church. Lutherans taught that people can be faithful to God without the aid of priests or formal rituals. The Lutherans lost property during the Counter-Reformation and many religious leaders left Hungary. Some returned to rebuild in the eighteenth and nineteenth centuries, but when the communists took over, Lutheran church properties were confiscated. After the return of religious freedom, the Hungarian Evangelical-Lutheran Church built more than five hundred places of worship, as well as schools and hospitals. Many Hungarian Lutherans have a cultural connection to Germany.

A Catholic priest greets churchgoers following a service on Christmas Eve in Nyíregyháza.

Jewish men read from the Torah, the first five books of the Bible, at a synagogue in Budapest.

Judaism

Jewish people were already living in what is now Hungary when the Magyars arrived more than a thousand years ago. When King Stephen took the throne, the Catholic Church imposed laws limiting freedoms for Jews. But later, the laws were eased and more Jewish immigrants arrived. In the centuries that followed, the Jewish people were either welcomed or persecuted, depending on which ruler was in power. In 1867, they were granted rights and freedoms equal to Protestants, freeing Hungarian Jews to establish schools, hospitals, and arts organizations. They took on important roles in agriculture and commerce. In 1895, a civil marriage law was passed in Hungary. Under this law, people were allowed to choose their religion freely and to marry without restrictions based on their religion. This gave Jewish Hungarians the same freedoms as Christian Hungarians.

But soon, the Hungarian government again turned against the Jewish people. After World War I, the government passed laws limiting Jewish involvement in education, government, and business to 5 percent of the population. The grandest Jewish house of worship in Hungary, the Great Synagogue in Budapest, was partially destroyed in anti-Jewish riots. Then, during World War II, more than half a million Hungarian Jews were killed.

After World War II, the surviving Hungarian Jews set to rebuilding. When the communist government took over, what little they had was taken away. Many Hungarian Jews emigrated. In 1991, the government abolished the anti-Jewish laws, allowing Hungarian Jews to reestablish schools, youth organizations, and prayer houses in their communities. With aid from the government, Hungarian Jews created the Hungarian Jewish Museum and restored the Great Synagogue, the largest synagogue in Europe. Today, about fifty thousand Jewish people live in Hungary, down from about nine hundred thousand a century ago.

Other Beliefs

In the last census, many Hungarians said they were nonreligious or did not belong to a particular church. A few thousand others, mainly in eastern Hungary, are Greek Catholic or Sunni Muslim. The Roma people may have practiced the Hindu religion more than one thousand years ago, but today, Roma who do practice a religion are mostly Christians. Many have converted to Pentecostalism in recent decades.

CHAPTER 9

Rich Traditions

THE NATIONAL PRIDE OF HUNGARIANS SHINES BRIGHTLY in their social customs and cultural life. While city style varies from village life, Hungarians live in a modern world shaped by a backdrop of rich traditions.

Opposite: **Many buildings in Hungary, such as this one in Pécs, are richly decorated.**

Architecture

Hungary is well known for its variety of architecture. From Roman ruins to award-winning modern buildings, Hungarian architecture brings history to life. The Romans settled in Pécs in the second century and built the largest Roman necropolis—a cemetery with elaborate monuments—outside of Italy. The Pécs necropolis is a vast arrangement of ancient burial chambers, marble tombs, and churches, all decorated with metalwork, sculpture, and paintings. When the Ottoman Turks later ruled Pécs, they built beautiful onion-domed mosques and elaborate Turkish baths. The largest synagogue in Europe, the Great Synagogue in Budapest, is built of red-yellow brick and rose-colored glass. Its two towers rise to the height of a fourteen-story building and are capped in copper.

Hungary is the site of nearly two thousand castles, many commissioned by Queen Beatrice of Aragon and built in Gothic and Renaissance styles. Under the reign of Maria Theresa, many churches and castles were built in a very ornate style called baroque.

Since the nineteenth century, Hungarian architects have developed modern styles of architecture that often include ideas from history and from Hungarian folk art. The Postal Savings Bank uses Hungarian floral motifs from folk art, and many of the buildings at the zoo in Budapest are built in the style of peasant

The Katona József Theater in Kecskemét was constructed in a highly decorated baroque style.

houses. Many more recent buildings have bold designs, including the Palace of Arts in Budapest and the Reök Palace in Szeged.

Art

Art in Hungary ranges from prehistoric stone carvings to contemporary sculpture. Art can be found everywhere, in small towns and large cities, in palaces, places of worship, museums, galleries, and marketplaces. The Museum of Fine Arts in Budapest displays art from all periods of European history. Also in Budapest is the Hungarian National Gallery, which features thousands of paintings and sculptures by Hungarian artists from the Roman conquest to the present.

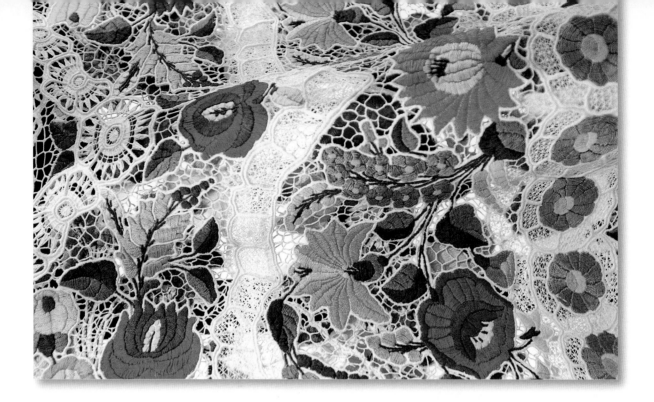

Hungarian embroidery most often depicts flowers and leaves.

The Vasarely Museum in Pécs showcases the work of Victor Vasarely, known as the grandfather of an international art movement called op art. Op art is short for "optical art," which is art based on visual tricks that make it appear like the paintings and sculptures are moving.

Hungary has a rich history of folk art. Hungarians are known for decorating everyday useful objects such as furniture and pottery in traditional designs of flowers, birds, and plants. Art and craft markets throughout the country feature traditional local folk art such as colorful porcelain teapots, painted dinner plates, and fine crystal. Hungarians are also known for their decorative wall hangings and traditional textile arts such as embroidery and lace making. Many villages have their own folk art specialty, and older, master artists pass their skills on to the next generation.

Music

Hungary is well known for classical music and unique folk music. Large concert halls regularly feature modern American and European popular music, and Budapest and Debrecen are known throughout Europe for their jazz scenes.

Two of Hungary's most famous classical musicians and composers are Franz Liszt and Béla Bartók. Liszt was born 1811. He began playing piano at age six, and by age nine he performed his first solo recital. Considered the finest pianist of his age, his talent brought him to the grandest concert halls in Europe. Although he spent most of his career away from Hungary, he worked with Hungarian musicians to build their musical institutions. He was the first president of the Academy of Music that opened in Budapest in 1875. Béla Bartók was one of the greatest composers of the twentieth century. He was one of the first people in the world to study in depth the rhythms and harmonies of eastern Europe's folk music. He blended traditional Magyar, Romanian, Slovak, Bulgarian, and Turkish music into his classical compositions. An opera called *Bluebeard's Castle*, a series of piano works called *Mikrokosmos*, and an orchestra piece called *Concerto for Orchestra* are some of his best-known works.

The most widely known of Hungarian folk music styles is Roma music, commonly called Gypsy music. The Roma first arrived in Hungary in the fourteenth century, and by 1800, they were the preferred musicians around the country, playing popular dances and songs for all kinds of social gatherings. Franz Liszt said that Roma musicians were Hungary's truest musicians, and their musical style influenced his compositions. Given that Roma were considered socially inferior, however, many Hungarian musicians disagreed with Liszt. Despite the conflicts between the Magyar and the Roma people, Hungarian audiences continued to appreciate Roma musicians.

Roma music has developed into many different styles. The kind of music many people think of when they hear the term *Gypsy music* is played with violins, sometimes clarinets, and an instrument called a cimbalom that has 125 metal strings and is played with a wooden or leather hammer. Another style of Roma

Roma musicians perform at a festival in 2014.

music relies less on instruments and more on singing, chanting, and tapping on everyday objects such as wooden blocks or cans. Since the 1970s, Roma have often used guitars with this style as well. Roma music varies from slow, bittersweet ballads about hardship to lively and enthusiastic songs.

Hungarian folk dancers often wear brightly colored costumes.

Dance

Hungarian dance houses, called *táncházok*, are found everywhere. Both the music and dances of the dance-house tradition come mainly from Hungarian-speaking communities in Transylvania, which is now in Romania. There are many kinds of folk dances from the different villages. Musicians and dancers at the dance houses in the cities learn them all. In the eighteenth century, the government hired Gypsy musicians to perform "recruiting music," or *verbunk*, for young men to dance to so they would get excited about joining the army. The *legényes* (young men's dance) is performed by one dancer at a time. The *csárdás* is performed by couples. It often begins slowly and builds to a fast and thrilling finale. The *csárdás* began gaining popularity in the early nineteenth century when Hungarians at balls wanted to do dances from their own country, not just dances from foreign places.

At the dance houses, people sometimes enjoy dancing the csárdás in their everyday clothes, but they might also wear traditional costumes. Costumes from some regions have full, bright-colored skirts that unfold when the dancers spin and twirl, while others are narrower and darker in color. Many people enter dance competitions and perform at events.

Literature

The National Széchényi Library of Hungary was founded in 1802 and houses more than ten million items. It features the first book ever printed in Hungary, *Chronica Hungarorum* (Chronicle of the Hungarians), which was produced in 1473 and relates the history of the region. The library also holds ancient texts once owned by King Matthias and Beatrice of Aragon.

One of the most widely admired Hungarian poets is Sándor Petőfi, who was born in 1823 and left home before finishing high school. He began writing poetry as a young man and once walked 140 miles (225 km) from Debrecen to Pest to get a book of poems published. Petőfi wrote a poem called "Nemzeti dal" (National Poem), which he recited to the crowds as the Hungarian Revolution of 1848 began. He died

Hungarian Wedding Traditions

Today, most Hungarian weddings are much like American weddings. Many ceremonies include Hungarian traditions, however. Hungarian couples must be married in a civil ceremony by a judge to make the marriage legal. When a couple wants a religious ceremony, often the entire wedding party follows the couple from the courthouse to the church for a second ceremony.

A time-honored custom was for the groom to go from house to house before the wedding to invite guests. Today, it is still considered polite for the couple to visit close family and friends and personally invite them to the wedding. While the couple is engaged, they wear their rings on their left hands. They switch the rings to their right hands after they are wed. The bride gives her husband either three or seven handkerchiefs because three and seven are lucky numbers. The husband gives his wife a small bag of coins. At church weddings, the bride and groom sit in chairs facing their guests. Family and friends take turns coming forward with songs, stories, and poems.

Some brides wear a traditional Hungarian wedding dress, which is brightly colored and heavily embroidered. But today, most wear white dresses and veils. One long-standing tradition at the wedding reception is the bride's money dance. During the money dance, people give gifts of money to dance with the bride.

Many of Magda Szabó's novels dealt with her family's history in Debrecen.

in battle just as the war ended in 1849 and remained popular after his death, especially among revolutionaries. Dozens of streets, parks, and bridges are named after him.

The only Hungarian to receive the Nobel Prize for Literature is Imre Kertész, who wrote a fictionalized memoir of his life as a fourteen-year-old Jewish boy in a Nazi concentration camp. Péter Nádas, another well-known author, wrote about communism. During the Soviet occupation of Hungary, Magda Szabó wrote about the difficulties women faced in a society controlled by men, and the government refused to allow her books to be published. Once the Soviets left, her books were published and she became famous for a story about a girl who set off on an adventure during World War II. Her work was turned into a popular television show in Hungary.

Sports

It is no wonder that with all the country's rivers, lakes, and thermal pools, Hungarians love to be in the water. Many towns and villages have easy access to lakes and rivers. City dwellers often visit the countryside to go swimming, boating, and fishing.

Hundreds of natural thermal springs have been made into swimming pools. On weekends, families flock to the pools to enjoy a day of swimming and soaking. There are several large pool complexes in Budapest. The Széchenyi Baths complex has eighteen pools, some of which are so warm that they are open year-round. It is common to see swimmers in the pools

People enjoy an evening soak at Széchenyi Baths in Budapest. Széchenyi is the largest thermal bath in Europe.

while snow lies piled up around them. The massive National Sports Pool is the home of the Olympic swimming and water polo teams. Besides swimming and water polo, Hungarian Olympians excel at kayaking and canoeing.

Hungarians are also active bicyclers. They take advantage of Hungary's nearly 1,400 miles (2,200 km) of bicycle trails, plus hundreds of miles of country roads. And they enjoy horseback riding as well. There is a Magyar saying that Magyars were "created by God to be on horseback."

Like their European neighbors, Hungarians—children and adults alike—love to play and watch soccer, known as football

Ferenc Puskás (in black shirt) fires a shot in the 1954 World Cup final against West Germany.

Into the Future

Hungary has a long history of being attacked and conquered. This has sometimes left the nation's most prominent buildings, such as Buda Castle, in ruins. Over the centuries, Hungarians have repaired the damage, often rebuilding with a different style of architecture.

One recent reconstruction stands apart. The Budapest Sports Arena was a main setting for large indoor sporting events. In 1999, a devastating fire burned the arena to the ground. When the replacement arena was completed in 2003, many people were shocked. People said the new, very modern building looked like an enormous UFO that had landed in the middle of Budapest.

The arena, named after László Papp, a Hungarian Olympic boxer, holds major sporting events, such as ice hockey, football, motocross, and tennis tournaments. It also hosts operas, circuses, and concerts by stars such as Lady Gaga and Beyoncé.

in much of the world. Backyards, ballparks, and schoolyards often ring out with cheers as fans root for their favorite teams.

Hungary's national football team in the 1950s was legendary. Nicknamed the Magnificent Magyars, the team recorded forty-two victories, seven ties, and just one defeat. The team won an Olympic gold medal and a World Cup championship. The most famous star of that team was Ferenc Puskás, who scored eighty-four goals in eighty-five games. The national football team's stadium, which seats fifty-six thousand fans, is named after him. Puskás and several of the other leaders of the Magnificent Magyars left Hungary after the 1956 revolution.

CHAPTER 10

Hungarian Style

U NTIL THE TWENTIETH CENTURY, LIFE IN HUNGARIAN cities was quite different than life in the country. Hungarians in the country held onto many traditional ways of dressing, making a living, and having fun. City life was more modernized, following the way of western European cities. But by the time Hungary reached full independence in 1990, country living had become more modernized. People in the country started wearing Western clothing, watching television, and using the Internet. Many left farms and ranches to work in cities and towns. Yet traditional foods, music, and holidays have not been forgotten and continue to be joyfully shared by all.

Opposite: **Dancing is a part of many Hungarian festivals.**

Food

The foods of Hungary are rich and varied and play an important role in the social lives of the people. The early Magyars grew grains, vegetables, and berries. When the Turks occupied Hungary, they introduced tropical fruits, nuts, coffee, and spices, including the highly prized paprika pepper. The reign of Austria over Hungary brought many new foods, such as sweet pastries, sour cream, dumplings, noodles, and sauerkraut. When Queen Beatrice married King Matthias, she charmed the court with delicious Italian foods such as sweet cream, butter, flavorful sauces, garlic, and ice cream.

Hungarian cooks appreciate their bounty and are known for many delightful dishes. Probably the most famous dish is Hungarian goulash, a hearty stew made from beef, onions, tomatoes, and green peppers, and spiced with paprika. Sometimes cooks add potatoes or carrots. Traditionally, goulash was cooked

Stews such as pörkölt (bottom) and goulash are popular in Hungary.

Hungarian Kiffles

Hungarian kiffles are a favorite cookie on holidays and other special occasions. They are not hard to make, but they look fancy enough to seem like they are! Have an adult help you with this recipe.

Ingredients

1 cup butter, softened

1 pound cream cheese

¾ cup powdered sugar

2 cups flour, plus extra for work surface

½ teaspoon salt

A jar of jam (apricot, raspberry, strawberry, or any favorite fruit)

Directions

Mix the butter and the cream cheese in a mixing bowl until they are fluffy. Gradually blend in ½ cup of powdered sugar, and then set the mixture aside. In another bowl, stir together 2 cups of flour and the salt. Pour the flour mixture into the butter and cream cheese mixture. Mix until the dough forms a soft ball. Place the dough in the refrigerator for at least an hour to make it easier to work with later.

Preheat the oven to 375°F. Divide the dough in half. Spread flour lightly on a cutting board or countertop. Flatten the dough and then use a rolling pin to roll it into long rectangles. Cut the dough into 2 x 2 inch pieces. Place a dab of jam in the middle of each square. With each piece, bring together two opposite corners and squeeze them closed.

Place the kiffles on a lightly oiled and floured cookie sheet. Bake them for 20 minutes, watching carefully to keep them from burning. When the cookies are done, remove them and place them on a cooling rack. After five minutes, sprinkle the cookies lightly with the rest of the powdered sugar. Impress your friends and enjoy Hungarian kiffles!

Yum!

Somlói galuska is Hungary's favorite cake. It is a delicate concoction of chocolate, walnuts, rum, and whipped cream. The mastermind behind this cake is Károly Gollerits, the longtime headwaiter at Gundel Restaurant, the most famous restaurant in Hungary. He dreamed up somlói galuska, and it was entered in the Brussels World's Fair in 1958, where it won the grand prize. People from all over come to Gundel's for the food, the art on the walls, the performers playing traditional music, and, of course, the nation's favorite cake.

in large pots outdoors, and many people still do cook outside for large gatherings and goulash contests. Hungarians say it is comfort food at its finest, especially in winter. In summer, many Hungarians delight in *gyümölcs leves*, a cold fruit soup made from apricots, cherries, or peaches.

Main dishes are usually made of potatoes, pasta, or rice mixed with a variety of meats or vegetables, with sour cream stirred in. Most dishes are spiced with sweet or spicy paprika or a combination of the two. Hungarian cooks also make a

School Lunch

One popular dish in Hungary is called *főzelék*. It is a thick vegetable stew made from potatoes, peas, beans, and carrots, and thickened with sour cream. The stew is often topped with hotdogs, sausages, or fried eggs. Besides being a meal commonly cooked at home, it is on nearly every school lunch menu. Főzelék fast-food restaurants can be found all around cities and towns.

number of unique pasta dishes, such as pasta with cottage cheese or roasted cabbage. Hungarian chefs also make unique breads. One favorite bread, made and sold in food carts and marketplaces everywhere, is call *lángos*. It is made from a special dough, fried in oil, and served with a choice of toppings, such as sour cream, sausages, or garlic dip.

Holidays

Through the year, beginning with New Year's Day, Hungarians get together with friends and family and celebrate. On New Year's Day, people often take to the streets, setting up tables and bringing great pots of food to share with neighbors and family.

A plane roars over
Budapest during an
air show.

Musicians and performers entertain and everyone toasts to the
New Year. Other national holidays include the Anniversary of
the Revolution of 1848, held on March 15. Celebrations begin
in Budapest at the National Museum, where poems by Sándor
Petőfi are read to the crowds. May Day is another important
holiday for Hungarians. It is a day devoted to workers. There
are parades, picnics, and, in Budapest, an international car race
and air show. On October 23, Hungarians honor the uprising of
1956 with parades and picnics.

Several Christian holidays are also public holidays in Hungary.
On Easter, many Hungarians go to church. The village of
Hollókő has a particularly large Easter celebration. The town is
decorated in flowers, and special foods are brought out, including a tasty gingerbread cake, an Easter favorite. Village artists
put their finely decorated Easter eggs on display. On November

Public Holidays

New Year's Day	January 1
Anniversary of the Revolution	March 15
Easter	March or April
May Day	May 1
Whit Monday	May
Saint Stephen's Day	August 20
National Day	October 2
All Saints' Day/All Souls' Day	November 1–2
Christmas	December 25

1 and 2, Hungarians hold a two-day national holiday to honor the dead. On All Saints' Day, many Hungarian Catholics go to church to honor all the saints. On November 2, All Souls' Day, public offices and buildings are closed so that family members can gather together to bring flowers to the graves of their ancestors and light candles there. In December, the holiday season begins on December 6 with the celebration of Mikulás (Saint Nicholas), when children receive presents of candy and cakes. Christmas Day is celebrated with family and friends. Children receive gifts,

At the Farsang celebration in Mohács, people parade in demon masks and fur robes. Some say the demons are meant to scare away winter. Others say the event began with trying to scare away the Ottomans.

and the table is spread with favorite foods such as stuffed cabbage; *halászlé*, a bright red fish soup; and chimney cake, a cake once served only to royalty. The ingredients include caramel, cinnamon, cocoa, coconut, and walnuts.

Celebrations

Hungarians love a holiday, and besides national holidays, many cities and towns offer up special festivities of their own. In Hungary, the midwinter holiday known as Carnival or Mardi Gras in other parts of the world is called Farsang. Many communities celebrate it with special foods, parties, and parades. The town of Mohács has the most famous Farsang celebration, with six days of parades filled with elaborate costumes, as well as concerts, parties, and dances.

Spring and summer bring many colorful outdoor festivals. On the first weekend in May, visitors flock to Lake Balaton for the opening day of boating season. In addition to sailboat races, there are concerts, parties, food, art fairs, and fireworks. The Budapest Spring Festival is the country's biggest cultural fair. The month-long festival features musicians from around the world performing in the city's major concert halls, such as the Hungarian State Opera House and the Palace of Arts. In late June, animal lovers from around the country come to Hortobágy National Park for the Shepherds' Festival and Equestrian Days. Visitors meet traditional herders and enjoy the country's largest

A man stands on the back of a horse during an equestrian event in the puszta.

Balancing Act

Children in Hungary play lots of games. Many enjoy video and online games, as well as card games, board games, soccer, and chess. But on playgrounds and at family gatherings, Hungarian hopscotch is a game children of all ages like to play together.

To play hopscotch, first a player takes a piece of chalk and draws a snail-like circle on the ground. Then he or she draws small boxes inside the lines. The first player takes a turn and tosses a small stone onto the circle. The player must hop on one foot to reach whatever box the stone landed on. If the player steps out of the lines, then the turn is over and another player begins. Once the player reaches the center, he or she turns and hops back to the start line. If the player makes it back to the start line, he or she tosses the stone backward over his or her shoulder. The player now "owns" whatever box the stone landed on, and no other player can hop on it. Other ways to make the game more difficult are to hop with eyes closed, hop backward, or balance another stone on a forearm or head. The winner is the player who owns the most boxes.

horse show, along with food, folk music, dance, and traditional crafts. In late July, history buffs visit Visegrád for the Palace Games. King Matthias's summer castle is in Visegrád, as well as several other castles, making it a perfect setting for jousting and fencing matches, archery competitions, and mock battles of medieval armies. Autumn brings countless harvest festivals across the country. A big favorite is the Goulash Festival in Szolnok, where seven hundred cooks compete for top awards in making Hungary's most famous dish.

Friends and Family

Hungarian families are close-knit. Even families who do not live in the same communities stay in touch and visit one another frequently. Family members rely on one another in many ways, and children and grandparents form special bonds. Today, most Hungarian families are small. The average Hungarian family has one child.

Friendships are also important to Hungarians, and most people have lifelong friends. Whether they live in the city or country, Hungarians love spending time with their family and friends. It is common to see people gathering to visit in cafés and restaurants and to hear the sounds of laughter, music, and lively conversation spilling into the streets.

Timeline

<table>
<tr><td colspan="2">HUNGARIAN HISTORY</td><td colspan="2">WORLD HISTORY</td></tr>
<tr><td></td><td></td><td>ca. 2500 BCE</td><td>The Egyptians build the pyramids and the Sphinx in Giza.</td></tr>
<tr><td></td><td></td><td>ca. 563 BCE</td><td>The Buddha is born in India.</td></tr>
<tr><td>The Roman Empire takes over Transdanubia.</td><td>1st century BCE</td><td>313 CE</td><td>The Roman emperor Constantine legalizes Christianity.</td></tr>
<tr><td>The Magyars cross the Carpathian Mountains and settle in what is now Hungary.</td><td>ca. 896 CE</td><td>610</td><td>The Prophet Muhammad begins preaching a new religion called Islam.</td></tr>
<tr><td>Stephen is crowned the first king of Hungary.</td><td>1000</td><td></td><td></td></tr>
<tr><td></td><td></td><td>1054</td><td>The Eastern (Orthodox) and Western (Roman Catholic) Churches break apart.</td></tr>
<tr><td></td><td></td><td>1095</td><td>The Crusades begin.</td></tr>
<tr><td>Andrew II signs the Golden Bull, creating parliament and limiting royal powers.</td><td>1222</td><td>1215</td><td>King John seals the Magna Carta.</td></tr>
<tr><td>Mongols invade Hungary and rule from Buda Castle.</td><td>1240–1242</td><td></td><td></td></tr>
<tr><td></td><td></td><td>1300s</td><td>The Renaissance begins in Italy.</td></tr>
<tr><td>The first Hungarian university is founded in Pécs.</td><td>1367</td><td>1347</td><td>The plague sweeps through Europe.</td></tr>
<tr><td></td><td></td><td>1453</td><td>Ottoman Turks capture Constantinople, conquering the Byzantine Empire.</td></tr>
<tr><td>Matthias is crowned king.</td><td>1458</td><td>1492</td><td>Columbus arrives in North America.</td></tr>
<tr><td>Reformation leaders convert many Hungarians to Protestantism.</td><td>1500s</td><td>1500s</td><td>Reformers break away from the Catholic Church, and Protestantism is born.</td></tr>
<tr><td>The Habsburgs gain control over parts of western Hungary.</td><td>1520s</td><td></td><td></td></tr>
<tr><td>The Ottoman Turks conquer Hungary.</td><td>1526</td><td></td><td></td></tr>
<tr><td>The Habsburgs take over Hungary; the Ottomans retreat.</td><td>1686</td><td></td><td></td></tr>
</table>

HUNGARIAN HISTORY

Maria Theresa of Austria makes social reforms.	**1740**
Hungary revolts against Austrian rule.	**1848**
Austria defeats the Hungarian uprising.	**1849**
Austria and Hungary create the Austro-Hungarian Empire.	**1867**
Austria-Hungary enters World War I.	**1914**
Admiral Miklós Horthy wrests control of the government from the Hungarian communists.	**1919**
Hungary enters World War II as a German ally.	**1941**
Germany invades Hungary.	**1944**
Hungary comes under the control of the Soviet Union.	**1945**
The Soviet Union quashes an uprising against communism.	**1956**
Hungary makes economic reforms, allowing some individual ownership of land and businesses.	**1968**
Hungary holds its first democratic elections.	**1990**
Hungary joins the European Union.	**2004**
The Hungarian parliament approves a new constitution.	**2012**
Europe faces a migrant crisis as hundreds of thousands of Middle Eastern and African refugees arrive.	**2015**

WORLD HISTORY

1776	The U.S. Declaration of Independence is signed.
1789	The French Revolution begins.
1865	The American Civil War ends.
1879	The first practical lightbulb is invented.
1914	World War I begins.
1917	The Bolshevik Revolution brings communism to Russia.
1929	A worldwide economic depression begins.
1939	World War II begins.
1945	World War II ends.
1969	Humans land on the Moon.
1975	The Vietnam War ends.
1989	The Berlin Wall is torn down as communism crumbles in Eastern Europe.
1991	The Soviet Union breaks into separate states.
2001	Terrorists attack the World Trade Center in New York City and the Pentagon near Washington, D.C.
2004	A tsunami in the Indian Ocean destroys coastlines in Africa, India, and Southeast Asia.
2008	The United States elects its first African American president.

Fast Facts

Official name: Hungary

Capital: Budapest

Official language: Hungarian

Budapest

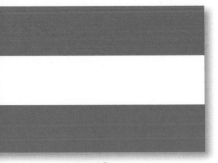

National flag

National anthem: "Himnusz" ("Hymn")

Type of government: Parliamentary democracy

Head of state: President

Head of government: Prime Minister

Area: 35,919 square miles (93,030 sq km)

Latitude and longitude
of Budapest: 47°29'N, 19°05'E

Bordering countries: Slovakia to the north, Ukraine to the northeast, Serbia and Croatia to the south, Romania to the east, Slovenia and Austria to the west

Highest elevation: Mount Kékes, 3,330 feet (1,015 m) above sea level

Lowest elevation: Near Szeged, 259 feet (79 m) above sea level

Average low
temperature: In Budapest, 25°F (–4°C) in January, 69°F (20°C) in July

Average high
temperature: In Budapest, 34°F (1°C) in January, 80°F (27°C) in July

Average annual
precipitation: In Budapest, 23 inches (59 cm)

Bakony Mountains

Budapest

Currency

National population (2014 est.):	9,919,128	
Population of major cities (2014 est.):	Budapest	1,744,665
	Debrecen	203,914
	Szeged	161,921
	Miskolc	161,265
	Pécs	146,581

Landmarks:
- ▶ *Buda Castle*, Budapest
- ▶ *Caves of Aggtelek National Park*, Aggtelek
- ▶ *Lake Balaton*, Siófok
- ▶ *Pannonhalma Abbey*, Győr
- ▶ *Széchenyi Baths*, Budapest

Economy: Hungary is a major manufacturing country, processing food and producing medicines and medical instruments, electronics and electronic parts, and luxury automobiles. Being centrally located, it is a major transportation hub and a popular tourist destination. Agriculture is also important. Major crops grown include wheat, corn, apples, sugar beets, and paprika peppers. Hungarian farmers also raise sheep, goats, cattle, and other livestock. The primary mining industries in Hungary are bauxite and coal.

Currency: The forint. In 2015, US$1.00 equaled 281 forints.

System of weights and measures: Metric system

Literacy rate: 99%

Teenagers

Ferenc Puskás

Common Hungarian words and phrases:

Szervusz	Hello or good-bye
Hogy van?	How are you?
Köszönöm, jól. És Ön?	Reply to "How are you?"
Mi a neve?	What's your name?
A nevem…	My name is…
Igen	Yes
Nem	No

Prominent Hungarians:

Béla Bartók (1881–1945)
Composer

Beatrice of Aragon (1457 –1508)
Queen

Lajos Kossuth (1802–1894)
Revolutionary and journalist

Franz Liszt (1811–1886)
Pianist and composer

Sándor Petőfi (1823–1849)
Soldier and revolutionary poet

Ferenc Puskás (1927 –2006)
Soccer player

Ernő Rubik (1944–)
Inventor and architect

Stephen I (ca. 970–1038)
First king of Hungary

To Find Out More

Books

- ▶ Guillain, Charlotte. *Hungary.* Chicago: Heinemann Library, 2012.

- ▶ Kalman, Bobbie. *Refugee Child: My Memories of the 1956 Hungarian Revolution.* New York: Crabtree Publishers, 2006.

- ▶ Kyuchukov, Hristo. *A History of the Romani People.* Honesdale, PA: Boyds Mills Press, 2005.

- ▶ Whiting, Jim. *The Life and Times of Franz Liszt.* Hockessin, DE: Mitchell Lane Publishers, 2005.

Music

- ▶ Lang Lang. *Liszt: My Piano Hero.* New York: Sony Masterworks, 2011.

- ▶ *Rough Guide to the Music of Hungarian Gypsies.* London: World Music Network, 2008.

- ▶ Schiff, András. *Schiff Plays Bartók.* New York: Savoy, 2009.

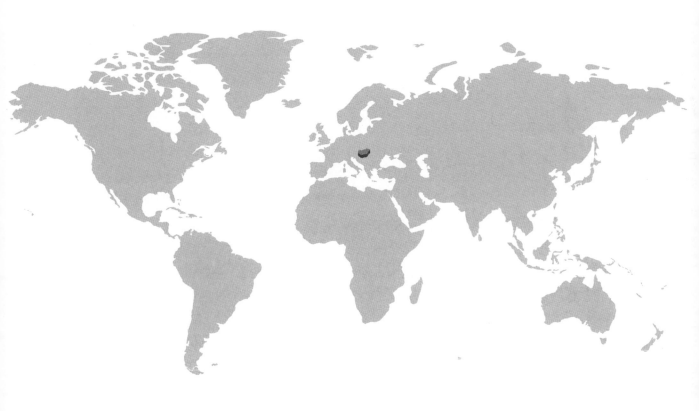

▶ Visit this Scholastic Web site for more information on Hungary:
www.factsfornow.scholastic.com
Enter the keyword **Hungary**

Index

Page numbers in *italics* indicate illustrations.

M

Magnificent Magyars football team, 115

Magyar people. *See also* people.
agriculture, 42, 117
Andrew II (king) and, 44
Árpád, 41, *41*, 42
Austro-Hungarian Empire and, 51
early settlements, 41–42, 83
foods, 117
Golden Bull document, 44
government and, 55
Habsburg Empire and, 48
Heroes' Square, 47, *47*
horseback riding, 114
influence of, 84
István Széchenyi, 50
Mongol invasion and, 83
music, 107, 108
names and, 84
population of, 66
religion of, 95
runic script and, 88

manufacturing, 20, 36, 37, *72*, 76, 77, *77*

maps. *See also* historical maps.
Budapest, 66
geopolitical, *10*
population density, *93*
resources, *75*
topographical, *25*

Maria Theresa, empress of Austria, 48–49, 87, 104

marine life, 27, 30, 74–75, *74*

marriage, 42, 64, 100, 111, *111*

Mátra Mountains, 19, 24

Matthias Church, 49, *49*

Matthias, king of Hungary, 44–45, 46, 47, 49, 110, 118, 126

May Day, 122

Mecsek Hills, 19, 20, 22

Mercedes-Benz company, 77

Middle Ages, 46, 49, 64

mining, 20, 36–37, 75, 76, 93

Miskolc, 20, 93

missionaries, 95

Mohács, 124, *124*

Mongols, 44, 49, 66, 83

mosques, 20, 49, 103

Mount Kékes, 19, 25

Museum of Fine Arts, 105

music, 14, 46, 107–109, *108*, 115, 122, 124, 133

N

Nádas, Péter, 112

Nagy, Imre, 59

names, 84

national anthem, 69

National Assembly, 44, 45–46, *62*, 65, 66, 67–68, *68*, 70, 71

national coat of arms, 64

national dish, 12, *13*

national flag, 64, *64*, 69

national flower, 35

national football team, 115

national holidays, 121–124, *121*

national minorities, 84–86

National Museum. *See* Hungarian National Museum.

national parks, 28, 33, 78, *92*, 93

National Sports Pool, 114

National Széchényi Library of Hungary, 110

natural gas, 76

Nazi Party, *54*, 55–57, 86

necropolis, 103

"Nemzeti dal" (Sándor Petőfi), 110

Nobel Prize, 112

nonreligious people, 95, 101

northern pike, 30

Norway, 37

nuclear power, 76

Nyíregyháza, *72*, 99

O

Óbuda (Old Buda), 66

oil industry, 76

Old Wooden Church, 20

Olympic Games, 114, 115

op art, 106

Orbán, Viktor, 65

Otto I, king of the Holy Roman Empire, 42, 95

Ottoman Empire, 46, 47, 48, 49, 103, 117–118, *124*

P

Palace Games, 126

Palace of Arts, 105, 125

Palatinus Strand, 15

Pálvölgyi Cave, 23

Pannonhalma Abbey, 96, *96*

Pannonian Sea, 19

Pannonia region, 40

Papp, László, 115

paprika farming, 9, 11–12, *11*

parliament. *See* National Assembly.

Pécs. *See also* cities.
agriculture, 25
architecture, 20, *102*, 103
economy and, 92–93
mining, 20
necropolis, 103
population of, 20, 93
Roman Empire in, 103
Vasarely Museum, 106

Pentecostalism, 101

peonies, 34, *34*

people. *See also* Magyar people.
borders and, 85
children, 126, *127*
civil liberties, 63, 65
clothing, 32, *109*, 111
early settlers, 39
education, 20, 95, 101
emigration, 89–91, *90*, 101

Protestantism and, 47
St. Stephen's Basilica, *94*
Stephen (king) and, 95–96, 100
Roman Empire, 40, 42, 66, 103
Romania, 79, 109
Roma people, 56, 86–88, *86*, 101, 108
Rubik, Ernő, 81, *81*, 133
Rubik's Cube, 81, *81*

Meet the Author

RUTH BJORKLUND ENJOYED A NATURE-FILLED childhood in rural New England. After school, and on weekends and vacations, she went hiking, rowing, and sailing.

She was first introduced to the sweet and savory cuisine of Hungary through her childhood best friend's mother. The friend's mother was Hungarian and rather shy, so conversations were usually limited. But her mother was not at all shy about sharing her cooking secrets. Her kitchen smelled like a spice shop, and her Hungarian goulash stew had no rivals.

When Bjorklund was twenty, she moved to Seattle, Washington. She holds a bachelor's degree in comparative literature and a master's degree in library and information science from the University of Washington. She worked as a children's and young adult librarian and then began writing books for young people. She has written on such subjects as endangered animals, medicine, Native Americans, immigration, and hydrofracking.

Bjorklund presently lives on Bainbridge Island, a ferry ride away from Seattle. She enjoys kayaking, sailing, camping, and traveling and watching the hummingbirds and spotted towhees at the birdfeeders on her deck.

Photo Credits